Spoiled Rotten:

American Children and How to Change Them

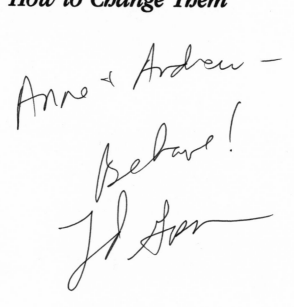

Anne & Andrew —

Behave!

J.B. Szor

Spoiled Rotten:

American Children and How to Change Them

Fred G. Gosman

BASHFORD & O'NEILL
MILWAUKEE
1990

ISBN 0-9627419-0-6   90-083252
                                                              CIP
FIRST EDITION

          3   4   5   6   7   8   9   10

Manufactured in the United States of America

Preface

*T*HIS BOOK GREW OUT OF MY INCREASING frustration with the behavior of young people. As I turned forty, I found that maintaining silence became more difficult.

The ethics of work and behavior that made our nation great are declining at an alarming rate. I am *amazed* by the underachievement of many of our young, as the easy way is becoming their chosen way.

And I am tired of seeing parents cater to their children's every whim, giving *so* much of themselves, yet frequently receiving so little in return.

It would be simple to give up, and claim that what worked for America previously is no longer applicable today. But that would be the easy way also.

For I still strongly believe in the essential strength and goodness of America, and feel that millions of Americans share this faith. Perhaps they are grandparents, who silently watch their grandchildren's behavior in horror. Perhaps they are parents, sensing something is wrong but not knowing what to do about it. And perhaps they are even children, aware that their own self-indulgence and apathy are downright unnatural.

I do know that to regain control we parents need to start communicating, working together, enforcing our standards and surrounding our children with more love but fewer things. Only when we begin to create change will America, and her parents and children, be confident once again.

It is in this spirit that I dedicate this book to my two children, Bobby and Mike.

—Fred Gosman

Table of Contents

Introduction

WHAT HAS BECOME OF OUR CHILDREN?

Remember when kids cut lawns rather than classes, and swore *by* their parents, not *at* them?

When proms didn't cost three hundred dollars, and Memorial Day wasn't just a picnic?

When people got their self-esteem from their home, not a class in school, and professional tennis players actually behaved?

Recently five children in Pennsylvania were discovered in a park using bags of grass clippings and sugar to operate a make-believe cocaine ring. As one official said, "Whatever happened to lemonade?"

Increasingly our kids get their self-concept from the number of their toys or the color of their Bugle Boys. Excellence is declining; thoughtfulness is for squares. And good manners is belching softly.

The very moral fabric of our society is endangered. Our mayors do drugs; many high schools have nurseries. Alcoholism has invaded the middle school, and date rape on campuses is completely out of control.

Many children today believe they were put on earth to play, that everything must be fun. Math and writing skills are considered irrelevant, needless in an age of calculators, and computers with spell checkers.

Recently a high school teacher assigned a Dickens novel as homework. One student inquired, "Is it on Beta?"

Graduating high school without a limo ride is an embarrassment for life. In college, our best and brightest believe that "life is a beach," and have made "party" a verb.

Even the political science students often don't bother to vote. One young man actually said during a recent survey that the way to boost voter turnout among teens was to "pay them," while another, when asked what made America special, answered "Cable TV."

When was the last time a neighbor's kid rang your doorbell and asked to shovel your walk or mow your lawn? And this in an age of power mowers and snow-throwers. Kids could easily earn ten dollars an hour, but they can't be bothered.

The "Gentleman's C" has invaded the middle school, and nationwide teachers encounter lack of effort, disrespect, and possible assault. Many ten-year-olds know the names of twice as many beers as Presidents. And as standards in general and student performance decline, formerly mediocre work becomes praised as excellent, with the result that our children are never pushed to discover their true potential.

How can we take back our kids, restoring respect, excellence, civility, and decent values, not to mention self-esteem? For these children of plenty are *not* happy. In a survey of students listed in Who's Who in American High Schools, an incredible twenty-eight percent said they had considered suicide. And these are some of our best.

Our kids need discipline, direction, love, and the gift of our time. Nothing more, nothing less. The battle has not been lost; their lives *can* be turned around. But the excessive gifts and toys must end, the unreasonable concern for their every thought and feeling must end, and acceptance of their mediocrity must end.

We must make crystal clear what our standards are, and clearly communicate and vigorously enforce consequences when they are breached.

It is time to remind our children that they are, alas, just children, that although they are exceedingly important, the earth still revolves around the sun.

Our youngsters deserve a life of substance, happiness, and value, just as we deserve their cooperation and civility. We cannot allow this to go on any longer.

The time for change is NOW.

SPOILING OUR KIDS

Nurseries of Plenty

*H*AVING A BABY IS PROBABLY THE GREATEST experience one can have. To actually see a little one born is both awesome and unforgettable.

Money suddenly becomes as disposable as the little tyke's diapers, and even penurious parents embark upon a spending spree to give their newborn absolutely everything *they* can possibly dream of.

Beaming parents desperately try to ensure that their child will have it better than they did, ignoring the strong possibility that they themselves turned out so well because they *didn't* have it all.

Life does change with a baby, of course, and many purchases are mandatory. A basic crib, rocker, changing table, dresser, mobile, hi-chair, playpen, bottles, stroller, etc., etc., are all necessary. But oh, how we often go overboard!

Especially intense parents start the process while the child is still in the womb. A California (of course) gynecologist and obstetrician runs Prenatal University where parents enroll to speak with their kids in the fifth month of pregnancy. Lucky dad gets to talk directly at mom's belly, while mom uses a megaphone-like device to address her midriff.

Hopefully these parental marvels remember to communicate with the kid *after* he's born!

Entire chains of specialty stores prey upon us, offering exclusive European designed children's furniture. As a result, our son's little table looks like a bright red slice of watermelon (mind you, a nice slice, but still a slice), and we own the largest and prettiest toy chests in the county.

An especially hot franchise in juvenile designer furniture is Bellini, importers of custom European products. Sample ads from their franchise kit illustrate the basic appeal to excess.

One, captioned "New Arrivals," claims that "when your plans for a newcomer include Bellini furniture, baby's homecoming is certain to be a treasured experience." Like you'd forget the arrival if you dared buy the crib at Sears!

Another ad, incredibly headlined "Starting Life with a Silver Spoon," declares that Bellini's furniture is the "certain choice when good isn't enough for your child and only the best will do."

How simple things would be if expensive furniture guaranteed a child's happiness.

Fashion in fact has invaded the baby biz. According to the executive director of the Juvenile Products Manufacturers Association, this "has been a godsend to the industry," adding over a hundred million dollars annually to sales.

One retailer notes that safety has peaked as an issue, and that "fashion has the spotlight." Let Toy and Hobby World tell it like it is. "Fashion today means more than a pretty comforter. Now soft goods makers are color-coordinating their product with hard goods and even with wallpaper manufacturers. Soft goods companies are also offering complete color-coordinated lines, including high chair covers, crib covers, and other products."

Simple and standard are now unacceptable; expensive and deluxe are the order of the day. The lamp shades have to match the sheets, and the beds have to look like cars. Strollers require hoods with ruffles, and clip-on pacifier holders come in various colors to match baby's outfits (really).

Even baby bottles are part of the act. Plain isn't good enough any more. Now we can go to our nearest store and be confronted with "designer nurser collections," baby bottles imprinted with character licenses or pretty designs. One brand promises a "color-coordinated cap ring and sealing disk," while a competing line reminds people to "look for our matching bib."

An Atlanta company even markets designer diapers in sixty-five different motifs (yes, sixty-five). Try the ones with the personalized valentine message—an absolute must for proper child development. These diapers cost about two bucks apiece, but don't stop there. For a little more you can imprint baby's name. As the company designer says, for a lot of people having kids today, "there's nothing they won't get for them."

Tiffany now retails sterling silver baby cups for eight hundred and fifty dollars. Cartier offers a six-piece bone china place setting for babies, selling "exceptionally well" at $267. What's next, mink coats at age two?

Some parents used to argue about who had the cutest kid. Now they debate whose nursery is the most fantastic:

"I just bought my child the best car seat," one parent brags. "It's anthropometrically designed" (whatever that means).

"Terrific," chimes in her friend. "I just picked up a swing that doubles as a car seat and carrier, and a crib puff in tones of yellow and blue."

"How nice," comes the icy reply. "By the way, did I tell you my baby's swing can run one hundred and fifty hours non-stop on two AA batteries? You still have to wind yours, don't you?"

"Yes," says the embarrassed friend, "but Linda's

18

swing is engineered to make a smooth, arc-like motion similar to my own, and her crib pillows play soothing lullabies."

Bested at last, the irate mom loses all control. "Listen, you, your kid's musical mobile isn't voice activated, the receiving blanket has two torn appliques, and your hi-chair cover doesn't even match."

And that's how the friends carry on!

If only raising a wonderful, considerate child was as simple as providing a fantasy nursery. Many parents go overboard because they know that kids often grow distant very quickly, and they want to capture precious moments while they can.

Certainly we don't do it for the kids, since babies don't care about this fluff and lace. And no wonder children start driving their parents crazy for "in" clothing—it's pretty hard to ignore the implications of their meticulously color-coordinated world.

And somewhere in this country, a child is being spanked because he messed on the designer quilt.

We stuff our playpens so full of toys, often there's hardly room for the kid. I can see the headline now: "Baby impaled on shape-sorter!" Obviously, children need all kinds of good toys during the early years. Unfortunately, many parents decide that more is always best.

Let's say our child needs a little play area to serve as a clubhouse. Why not find a really big box and decorate it with pictures of Ernie and Bert? The child and his friends could even do the coloring. Instead, we shell out a hundred and fifty bucks for the unassembled, prefabricated wonders found in our toy stores.

And what is this mania for fancy swing sets? How will the youngster possibly enjoy the equipment at the playground or the nursery school if his gym set at home is nicer?

Many different companies market to these young swingers, with prices often starting over three hundred dollars. Remember when a swing set didn't have to be "closely attuned to children's social and physical needs"? As long as the swing was the right height, the kids were in heaven. Now, the more gymnastic options available, the better the parent.

One mom quoted in Parents magazine related her tale of woe: "As long as we were buying a swing set we thought we'd get the best one, so we went for the deluxe, 100% redwood, gymnastic yuppie model. It looked beautiful in the backyard, but the kids didn't gravitate to it. They preferred the neighbor's $79.95 metal tubing swing set."

Our garages are stuffed with countless children's vehicles, even though they can only ride one at a time. No wonder we can't find the mower. Scooters, mini-wheels, big-wheels, in-between wheels, coupes, 4 by 4's, and 8 by 8's; they're all here.

But truly loving parents will give their children one of the battery-powered cars now on the market. Sure, the kids won't use their legs to pedal, but don't worry, their muscles will probably develop fine anyway.

These cars are new over the last few years, and cost anywhere from a hundred and fifty to two hundred and fifty dollars. Some come with Goodyear tires, others with fold-down windshields and working headlights. At all times keep in mind the severe psychological implications of giving a car without a play CB or cellular phone.

To parents who require the very best, even these hot-shot vehicles might appear pedestrian. Don't let your child be caught driving in just *any* car—get your wheels from Prestige Mini Motors. Really.

Toys R Us ran a full-page ad one recent Christmas for Prestige's battery-powered cars. The headline titillated readers with the claim of the "lowest sticker price ever on these luxury imports," and the ad copy implored parents to "hand your child the keys to a European flair sportscar."

Of course, buying these cars doesn't provide enough fun, so be prepared to shell out for the play stop sign, the do-not-enter sign, the pretend gas pump, and the working stop-and-go light. What the heck, they just add eighty bucks, and we have to protect our investment!

Kiddie electronics is also booming, despite the fact

that our kids will grow up and drive us crazy with loud stereos and boom boxes.

Sony recently introduced its "My First Sony Collection," personal stereos and boom boxes for the discriminating punk toddler. The company brags that its collection is "scaled down for easy operation by kids," with smaller controls that "make them perfect for pint-sized hands." Who said that the playpen is too early to learn brand loyalty?

Computer education toys abound, as mom and dad do everything possible to give their children every educational advantage. This despite the fact that the kids watch Sesame Street eight times a week, and are educationally advanced for their age.

Remember the Speak and Spells from the past? Anyone have kids who used these for more than a few days? We should really call them Speak and Spends. The latest generation of computer products makes glorious beeps, and provides wonderful, supportive messages to our children as they master their skills.

Does any of this work? Aren't test scores *still* declining, despite the availability of new technology? And if preschoolers master skills at home, might they not be bored when they enter school and need to rehash the stale material?

And folks, we're raising a whole generation who thinks learning must be fun (the new F word). The truth is that our children will encounter many boring teachers. They will still need to pay attention and learn, a task made more difficult by these user-friendly machines.

Birthday parties are also times for excess. Remember when a piece of cake and a game of pin the tail on the donkey were all that was required? Most of the kids had a great time, and even remembered to say thank you when leaving. No longer.

Birthdays now are staged events. Parents openly vie with one another to create the most talked-about happening. Take the entire nursery school to the circus and out to eat afterwards? Go for it—so what if they're still stuffed from the cotton candy! But don't take the kids to the local video game parlor. If you're lucky, only half of these well-behaved little darlings will ask for more quarters when they run out.

Have you noticed the obsession we now have with party favors? Why can't this generation learn that the birthday boy gets all the attention? It used to be you could give the children a cheap, plastic yoyo and they'd be content.

Now, some parents go crazy trying to come up with the hit item that will have the guests (and their parents) talking about the party for months. Inevitably, even these favors will still be broken or lost within minutes, but it doesn't seem to matter.

True story. I was driving the children home from my five-year-old's party and one of the kids in the back seat whispered to his neighbor, "They must be poor. We didn't get favors."

Kiddie culture is an important part of modern parenting. Most three-year-olds are on a first-name basis with every animal at the zoo. And I've just learned of a suburb where children are placed in foster homes if they miss "Sesame Street Live."

Souvenirs are now mandatory, an entitlement of the young. Take a kid to a circus, and he *has* to get the clown mask. It's not enough that you spent ten bucks apiece on tickets, five dollars for parking, and six more on three small Cokes (two of which spilled).

We parents often try to give our children just about everything *we* can dream of. In doing so, we destroy the thrill and excitement that only result when treats are received *rarely*. Our children become jaded and unappreciative of all that they have, and a style has been established whereby they *expect* to get all that they want.

I'm guilty of this, and perhaps so are you. This surfeit of possessions is robbing our children of innocence and surprise, and must be reversed before our kids begin to believe they are entitled to even more.

For when we fulfill all our children's wishes, they have nothing left to dream of. And the wonder of life is gone.

POINTS TO REMEMBER

- Love should be the mainstay of a nursery, not fashion.

- Children's backyard playsets should have no more than fourteen separate activities.

- A deluxe, battery-powered vehicle should not cost more than the family car.

- Just because we can afford to buy something for our children doesn't mean we should.

- The number of vehicles our children have should not exceed the number owned by the U.S. Army.

- We shouldn't complain about our youngsters becoming punk rockers if we give them personal stereos for their third birthday.

- Computer enhanced education skills are not a great benefit if as a result all human teaching is perceived as boring.

- Parents should not spend more than half a year planning their kids' birthday parties.

- Kids will not die if they let the birthday boy get all the attention.

Toys, Toys, Toys

*A*CCORDING TO THE PRESIDENT OF THE TOY Manufacturers of America, there are approximately one hundred and fifty thousand toys on the market. Many adults seemingly are hellbent to provide every single one for their pampered girl or boy wonder.

Even parents who don't believe in excess discover that their shy and acquisitive little toddlers easily master the complex psychological skills to make them silly putty in their hands. As a result, we are a nation of toy chests with hernias and multi-page wish lists. Receiving what is wanted has become a natural law of childhood.

How successful are the kids? Only 13.4 billion dollars worth. That's the amount spent on toys at retail in 1989. Not surprisingly, toy manufacturers don't release data on the dollar amount of the toys that are actually *played with*.

The culprit of course is television. Clever advertisers use TV to entice our children into asking for overpriced nonsense. The three-year-old catches a pitch for a new dollie, and suddenly the family has a new member. Think of what it must have been like in the good old days before television.

Alas, TV is here to stay. Kids aged two to five watch an average of four hours a day, far and away more time than they spend daily with their fathers, and often even their mothers. In case you're wondering why all our standardized test scores have been heading south, consider that by the time a child is eighteen, he's watched fifteen thousand hours of TV, whereas he's been in classrooms for eleven thousand hours.

As a result of this tube torture, our kids sit through thousands and thousands of slick commercials, all claiming to portray the hottest products of the decade. In 1989, toy manufacturers spent close to four hundred million dollars on advertising. These companies are not stupid—if their "informational messages" weren't working, they'd allocate resources elsewhere.

One researcher pegs at nineteen the number of commercials kids see per cartoon hour. A child watching four hours of Saturday morning cartoons is bombarded by seventy-six commercial messages. That's almost *four thousand a year*.

Is it reasonable to expect toddlers and young kids to successfully defend themselves against this multimillion dollar assault? All these commercials are slickly done, with music that is fetching and lighting that is perfect. They employ sophisticated photographic tricks, and depict unrealistic scenes. All the toys have been successfully assembled for the camera (a minor miracle), and the kids are smiling incessantly, even when their battleships are sunk.

Why does a society that went to the moon allow its kids to be manipulated like this? Many European governments routinely protect their children from this exploitation. How can toddlers really be expected to accurately judge the play value of a toy based upon a seductive, thirty-second commercial? They can't vote till eighteen. What makes them prudent toy analysts at four?

Yet whenever toy officials defend this commercial rape of our children, they pontificate about our kids' innate sense of value, and the impossibility of "fooling" a three-year-old. Hogwash, isn't it? We fool them every day.

And why don't these ads list *prices*? Even if we assume kids are mature enough to make good decisions, how can they do so without knowing a toy's price? Most adults would never buy anything without knowing its cost, and neither would toy marketing executives.

Wouldn't it be wonderful if the manufacturer disclosed a recommended list price at the end of the ad?

Individual stores would still price the item as they wish, and discounters would still be lower than their competition. But the children would at least have a frame of reference.

Added to the impact of television commercials is the growth of licensing, or putting the likeness of favorite characters on items as various as toys, T-shirts, and lunch boxes.

This is new. Used to be, only characters with long-term, proven track records could be licensed. Now, the licensing and marketing come first, and the show is the afterthought. According to one source, worldwide sales of licensed products have grown six-fold in the last ten years, to approximately $60 billion *annually*.

Read the trade press, and you'll quickly see the dominant role of licensing. At a recent LICENSING EXPO, not one, not two, but five thousand and one hundred marketing executives showed up. That's a lot of smart people trying to get our kids into our pocketbooks. No wonder we're losing.

Remember back a few years when we became a California Raisin society? Yes, the little guys were cute, but just because whimsical figures have appeal, why is it essential that their likenesses be on everything? Do we really need California Raisin pillow cases, sheets, sleeping bags, sweatshirts, underwear, umbrellas, finger puppets, watches, shoelaces, pajamas, squeeze bottles, etc?

Why can't we give kids more time to enjoy the licensed products we gave them *last* month? We hope to instill fundamental, long-term values, and yet we often allow them to chase fad after fad.

And what will they do when the license is no longer hot? Play the California Raisin Board Game, new from Milton Bradley? Not on your life.

In the cruelest form of exploitation, our kids now watch program-length commercials, TV shows specifically designed to sell toys. The stations don't allow ads for a specific program's toys to run during the show itself, but this is no big deal. The entire half-hour is one long commercial.

This is a new development. Thank innocent-looking Strawberry Shortcake and He-Man for starting it all. The FCC used to frown upon this kind of programming. But in the eighties this changed. According to one estimate, in one recent year there were "at least seventy programs that are little more than thirty-minute commercials for toys."

The people who design these shows are after dollars, not Emmys. Each program features scores and scores of heroes and villains, the better to sell lots of action figures, each sold separately (whatever happened to sets?). Count on the hero to drive a fancy, gimmicky vehicle ideally proportioned for reproduction in plastic, and to have a hide-out or headquarters that costs at least thirty dollars at retail.

Now toy manufacturers actually create much of our children's programming. As Peggy Charren, President of Action for Children's Television, a child-advocacy group, recently said, "Where is it written that Mattel should control the decision making in programming for children's TV?" Or, as a Vice President of CBS's children's programming stated, "It's the tail wagging the dog when the merchandising is put first and the show is designed to sell it."

Nor are the themes of the toys often much better than the messages of the commercials. Do you happen to have a little toy basketball hoop in your house? Remember when it didn't require a breakaway rim?

Now practically every backboard shows three-year-olds dunking with abandon. Get this recent Toys R Us ad: "Your little star can practice the bone-crushing dunks that made you a legend." It even refers to our kids as "future pros." Our children grow up thinking of sports as "showtime," with dunking and trick shots taking priority over practice and teamwork.

Some companies even market their toys as if they will become our children's friends. Roadmaster peddles a tricycle that comes with a detachable Minnie Mouse doll. As the ad says, "Now a cycle comes with a friend to play with," Playskool's "Kid Sister" doll is "a true friend," and its blankie, a "Nap Pal."

Isn't there some danger that our children of plenty will substitute these "friends" for the human kind?

Parents vie with one another in an intense scramble to obtain the hottest toys first. The home with the only Nintendo set in the neighborhood crawls with activity, even if the neighborhood kids dislike the child who lives there. These children practically become members of the family.

This doesn't last long, however, since they too will get a set. The unpopular child will once again be friendless. And eventually he will wise up, and realize that being unpopular is a cleaner feeling than being used.

Remember the mania over Cabbage Patch Dolls a few years back? These were advertised heavily, and every girl just *had* to have one. Since supply was short, some children had to go without. That was fine, as long as these kids weren't ours.

Many parents went absolutely crazy to find these ugly beauties. Through practice they memorized the phone number of every local toy retailer, as they pleaded with clerks for inside information on their inventory outlook. Some truly addicted adults travelled to nearby cities, hoping to find a Cabbage Patch in a cabbage patch.

Moms and dads would rearrange their schedules so as to be at the toy store exactly when a shipment was expected to arrive. Some even put out frantic pleas over community radio shows. The dolls became an obsession, finding one a test of their worth as a parent or grandparent.

This general mania for hot toys is especially ironic since the fashion nature of the toy business is well known. According to the editor of <u>Playthings</u> magazine, a toy trade journal, ninety-five percent of all new toys are not on the market two years after introduction. Last year's hit is almost always this year's closeout.

Look at Kay-Bee Toy and Hobby, a national toy retailer. Although Kay-Bee sells current toys, it also has many closeouts, once popular items acquired on the cheap.

Like a toy cemetery, here are all the hot toys of yesterday—the Rambo figure our children just had to have, the Atari and Lazer Tag Sets, the Pound Puppies, and the Teddy Ruxpin and Pee Wee Herman dolls. Cycle after cycle of scorned product silently cry out for renewed popularity, at a fraction of the original price.

But our children can't be bothered. They walk past their fallen heroes as if they were strangers, and march to the rear of the store to buy the hot toys of today at full price.

Year after year it's the same. Our children *have* to have a toy, so we go out and buy it. Sure enough, in a matter of weeks (if not days) it sits in a state of permanent disuse. Although we generally don't throw good money after bad, and usually believe in cutting our losses, we can't bring ourselves to say "no" to a hot toy.

Some folks get so caught up in the toy-buying frenzy that they allow their children to wear clothes licensed by toy manufacturers.

Good old Tonka Corporation, the maker of long-lasting trucks and other vehicles, is leading the way. K-Mart recently retailed an entire collection of Tonka-licensed shirts and pants, "traditional fun clothes for the kid who's Tonka Tuff" (God forbid your kid wouldn't qualify). Your lucky child could be part of the Tonka Tuff Club, or even the Tonka Naval Academy. And he can think of toys every time he gets dressed. Terrific.

In fact, Toys R Us seems to think that adults are so wild about toys that prices are irrelevant. They often run full-page ads, targeted to adults, which don't list prices. I've never before seen a retailer do this. Each ad features just a single toy, and not all the showcased items are expensive. But absolutely no pricing information is given.

One recent ad featured the Lionel "Gold Rush Special," a three-car train set. Aren't people entitled to know they are gazing upon a gift which costs $249.99? Can you imagine showing the picture of the toy to your child and *then* discovering the price?

Basic versions of toys are often no longer good enough for our children. Girls now compare dollies not on looks but on breadth of vocabulary. One new doll talks when her hair is brushed, and another actually stains its diapers in two realistic colors (really).

Children of both sexes rate their tennis games not by their scores but by the expense of their rackets. Kiddie kitchen sets need to have "real" cooking sounds, and require play coffee makers, dust busters, and blenders, despite the cost to our wallet and the child's imagination. And if we put our foot down and set limits, a doting grandparent will often come out of the woods to make the child's dreams come true.

Haven't we allowed our children to be manipulated by toy companies long enough? Are any of us strong enough to "inflict" an unwanted chemistry set or microscope on children demanding hot, licensed merchandise? Can't we give them gift certificates for future fun rather than toys that die?

Many children have *never* been denied a toy they asked for. As a result, they gain no experience in handling disappointment. It is time for our kids to learn that gratification can sometimes be deferred.

Most assuredly, occasionally exposing them to disappointments will help more than all the hot toys manufacturers have to peddle.

POINTS TO REMEMBER

- Wish lists should never be more than six items long.

- A society that doesn't restrict commercial exploitation of its children shouldn't claim to love them.

- Commercials targeted to children that don't disclose prices are inherently deceptive.

- Not always buying children the toys they want takes more love than buying them.

- The more licensed merchandise we buy, the more obsolete our previous purchases.

- Program-length commercials are an obscenity, and should be dramatically curtailed.

- Dolls that wet should always be cheaper than ones that don't.

- Desperately trying to find a hot toy for our children should never take more than half our waking hours.

- At least once a year we should buy a toy that isn't the deluxe version.

- What's good for Mattel and Nintendo isn't necessarily good for America.

- Children who always get what they want will want as long as they live.

Fashions,
Tantrums, and Treats

WOULDN'T IT BE WONDERFUL IF THE PRETTY nursery and bulging toy chests produced cooperative, respectful children?

Instead, like an immutable law of physics, usually the more children have, the worse their behavior. And instead of correcting the situation through discipline, often we parents continue to shower clothes, attention, and treats on our misbehaving young.

Even our youngest now need to be dressed to the nines. Nike recently placed an ad for tiny, down-sized tennis shoes and pants. The target market—"Those who wet instead of sweat."

And Nike is not alone. Babies can pee in their very own Ocean Pacifics. The GAP now operates GAPKIDS stores, while ESPRIT has ESPRIT KIDS. Pretty soon we'll be able to tell where a toddler shops just from his "look."

Some parents give their children *exclusive* fashion

control. Says the owner of a Manhattan shoe store, "even eighteen-month-olds are having a voice. They go over and choose which shoes they like. They're like little customers."

But sadly this phenomenon is not limited to the coasts. An article in a midwestern newspaper reported the fashion insights of local children. A seven-year-old honored lucky readers with her philosophy of fashion, while the mother of an eight-year-old stated that her daughter had "been dressing herself since she was three. That's when I lost any impact."

All this indulgence and independence hasn't brought about much thoughtfulness and kindness. In fact, our children have developed the notion that they are *entitled* to just about anything, whether it be clothing, toys, or treats. And so often when discipline is called for, we respond with further indulgence.

Give a child a toy and we frequently won't hear a thank you. And regardless of how much he has, he still will ask, "What is there to do?"

Talk about indulging instead of disciplining, my wife witnessed this scene: A mom and her two-year-old were having ice cream. After each bite, the child dropped his spoon on the floor. After picking up the spoon and cleaning it four times, the mom said, "If you drop the spoon again, I'll throw the ice cream away." Sure enough, the utensil fell to the floor again. Mom said she would throw away the ice cream, but when the child began to cry, she gave him "one more chance."

I saw a similarly hilarious confrontation. A mother and son were in line at Burger King. Whoppers happened to be on special for ninety-nine cents, and the conversation went like this:

"John, I'm having a Whopper," the mother said. "I suppose you want one too?"

"I don't feel like a Whopper today," came the reply. "I want the chicken sandwich."

The mom sensed her pocketbook was in trouble. "Come on, Johnny, it's cold outside. Beef will keep you warm."

No luck. "I want the chicken sandwich," the young gourmand repeated. "And large fries."

"Honey," the worried mother continued, "we're having chicken for dinner tonight. Wouldn't you like a nice Whopper?"

Needless to say, the mom lost. But this incident does show how we cater to our kids. Mom will eat the Whopper to save a few cents, but she can't force the kid to have one, even though Johnny often eats burgers and hasn't finished a chicken sandwich in his young life.

The simplest of kiddie problems fills us with indecision. Recently a lady wrote to an advice columnist, complaining that her scared three-year-old child had been sleeping with her and her husband for the last eighteen months. The lady claimed that this was "ruining my marriage" (surprise, surprise), but didn't have the heart to have the child sleep in her own room. Gosh, what a world-class quandary! The daughter might have to cry herself to sleep for a night or two. Better to ruin a marriage, right?

Or look at what happens when a young child runs into the street without looking. Serious stuff. This is the one time we have to take our child's hand and slap it repeatedly till he or she has the concept. Yet often we will see parents "lecturing" rather than disciplining. Since the last "talk" didn't do the job, why would this one?

If the traffic doesn't take care of the difficult child, perhaps we've all been tempted to kill him in the supermarket. The confrontation normally begins near the entrance, when mom gently and tenderly places precious little Brad into a sitting position in the shopping cart. Almost instantly, the lad is standing. Mom puts down the can of peas, puts Brad back in place, and reminds him to stay seated.

One minute later, the little tyke is up again. This time mom notices not quite as quickly, and gently lectures on the catastrophes that can befall a standing toddler. Within seconds Brad is on his feet again. This time mom yells. Next time she spanks. All to no avail.

When she reaches the checkout, the kid is doing

cartwheels on the Wonder Bread and handstands on the Florida grapefruit.

Even kids like these get rewarded with candy as they check out of the grocery store—though it often takes twenty minutes to decide what to get. Sometimes there are even "No Candy" aisles, where managers have been "kind" enough to tell shoppers that here, at least, they won't need to confront hundreds of candies.

What an indictment that we need a store manager to do our dirty work. Why can't we just tell our children "no"? Why do naughty children deserve a thing? If once we denied the treat, they'd behave.

Maybe the shopping cart is such an unpleasant experience because our children have always been entertained when they've had to sit. This began when, through the best of intentions, we bought the activity sets for their hi-chairs. How can we expect our youngsters to actually stay put if they don't have a sliding Pluto to divert them?

Likewise with the toys we provide for their travels. One entertainment center for the car seat has a steering wheel, working horn, play stick shift, and a clicking directional signal. And now all our deluxe vans have TVs and VCRs.

And what about all those playgrounds in the fast food restaurants? I know that young moms especially enjoy sitting with a friend while the kids are playing.

It's a touch of heaven (and quiet) amidst a very demanding schedule. But the danger is that the kids will never learn to sit still, and be dismissed to the play area with the first fidget.

Children are seeing more and more of fast food restaurants. Almost two million meals daily. If our kids go to a McDonalds or Burger King once a week, that's over two hundred and fifty visits by age five. That's a lot of unfinished burgers.

We often allow our children to decide which restaurant we frequent. Amazing, isn't it? They'll probably act horribly, and just nibble at their meal, but we defer to the little Burger kings regardless. And two kids can *never* agree on a restaurant. Just as you pull into the parking lot, one little ingrate will always inform you, "I hate this place."

Watching children dine in these restaurants is not a pretty sight. One child always believes the other kid is on his side of the bench, and that someone else's fries are larger. Children roam around freely, as if it is the responsibility of fellow diners to watch them.

Since kids' behavior is often so poor, why reward them with trinkets sold in the restaurants? Shouldn't eating out be a sufficient treat? Yet the sad truth in many families is that we have to order a "Happy Meal" in order to have a happy meal.

Just walk through McDonalds sometime and count all the "Happy Meal" boxes. Included inside each is a trinket. McDonalds spends a fortune peddling this gimmick on Saturday morning TV, with commercials featuring Ronald leading the "Happy Meal Players" in song.

McDonalds is not alone in selling trinkets. Hardees referred to fanatical fans of its California Raisins as "grapees," and during its popular promotion actually set up a twenty-four-hour hotline in Atlanta to answer questions about availability. As one food analyst commented, "If you can't lure them in with food, lure them in with a stuffed animal." Can it be long before toy stores dish up burgers?

Gimmicks can also be found in all the kiddie cereal boxes, and an anthropologist could have a field day. Of course there's the expected nonsense items, like dinosaur rings, alien detector fingerprint kits, and glow-in-the-dark talking skulls. But there are also some surprises.

Trix, which claims that "eating right helps you feel good and grow strong," gives away free M&Ms. They will go well with orange juice!

And Post's Natural Raisin Bran once provided the rare privilege of ordering a cassette featuring songs by our good friends, The California Raisins. Cost was "only $4.99," and the tape featured "I Heard It on the Grapevine," as well as "other classics."

But two contests appear rather shocking. Quaker's Life cereal offers a seemingly innocent promotion.

Kids submit two pictures of themselves, and the child who has both the "yuckiest" and "sweetest" face will win a United States savings bond to help pay for college. No problem here, cute contest. How much money do you think the winner gets? $100? $500? $1,000? Would you believe $50,000? That's a big number for a kid, isn't it? Know what second gets? Just $2,000.

But I've saved the best for last. You will think I am making it up, but sadly I am not. Ralston Purina has come up with an outrageous premium for its The Real Ghostbusters (remember when cereals weren't named after TV shows?).

On the front of each package is a child holding a dollar bill. The nearby inscription reads, you guessed it, "Instantly Win $10,000." The entire back of the box doesn't mention the cereal, but just promotes the contest.

Can you imagine Ralston Purina doing this to our kids? If the correct Super Cash Card is in the box, Jessica is rich! I can see children buying the cereal just for the contest and pouring out the contents. How can we keep our kids in dinosaur rings if this is permitted?

All the possessions and lost disciplinary opportunities create toddlers used to getting their way. Almost from birth, they've received everything they've asked for, and perhaps *never* have been effectively disciplined. As the fashionably dressed youngsters walk to school for the first time, they must feel that their utopian existence is bound to continue.

Is it any wonder that first grade teachers are such notoriously poor sleepers?

POINTS TO REMEMBER

- Parents who give children everything shouldn't complain that their kids are spoiled.

- Toys belong at McDonalds like burgers belong at Toys R Us.

- Parents who never remove their children from a restaurant either have saintly children or no regard for fellow diners.

- Children who make all of their clothing decisions have a GAP in their upbringing.

- We should not be able to tell where toddlers shop just by seeing their "look."

- Children who don't say thank you when receiving a toy should always have it immediately taken away.

- The more boredom killers we provide our kids, the more they will need.

- Children who run into the street without looking require our strongest discipline.

- Never give misbehaving kids treats in the grocery store.

- The date our children first learn sportsmanship is more important than the date they make their first basket.

Nintendo Finger
and Other Materialisms

*U*NSATED BY THE ATTENTION AND TOYS OF their first five years, acquisitive grade schoolers join with their parents to continue the buying spree. Trucks and cars are gradually replaced by video games, with "Nintendo Finger" becoming the new American rite of passage. And instead of buying $7.95 dresses for Barbie, young ladies can be found at Benetton, purchasing expensive clothing for themselves.

Nintendo is everywhere, already in over half of all homes with children, despite the fact that Americans invested billions in Atari machines a few years ago that became obsolete within eighteen months. Not to mention Intellivision. Intelliwhat?

Money is no object in satisfying the video dreams of today's young. Put together the video game set, a variety of game cartridges, specialty joysticks (a must), and the deluxe cart to keep all this stuff organized, and we're looking at no small change. In

1989, kids spent over ten billion dollars on video games.

As all parents know, *each* child must have absolutely all of the hot cartridges. Contrast this for a second with how our adult neighbors share certain items, like wheelbarrows and fertilizer spreaders, to save a few bucks. Apparently children can't be asked to sacrifice similarly.

Nintendo of course doesn't endorse the concept of sharing, and in fact encourages children to profit off the purchases of their friends. Regular readers of Nintendo Power magazine are rewarded with a special pin when they get their friends to subscribe. How much better for a child and his good buddy to share the magazine, and jointly discuss game strategy.

What a wonderful gimmick this magazine is. Even if the kid has twelve friends who subscribe, he will ask for it right after he brings the main set home, the conversation usually going something like this:

"Dad, I want to subscribe to Nintendo's magazine. It's just $15.00." (This generation usually uses the word "just" immediately before any dollar figure less than one hundred).

"Whoa," comes the startled reply. "I just spent two hundred and ninety dollars on this stuff. Why do you need something else?"

"I just do, dad," your son continues. "That's how you learn to play the games really well."

"Hold it a minute," the dad responds, getting red in the face. "You mean I worked overtime to get you these games and they don't come with instructions?"

"Of course they include instructions, dad," comes the reply. "Don't be silly. But just the *simple* instructions. Every game has secrets, and you have to subscribe to the magazine to find out what they are."

Dad caves in, and writes the check. He tries to hide from his son a sudden hand gesture that he makes at the game unit.

"What are you so upset for, dad?" asks the video maven, "and why is your middle finger raised?"

"Son," the now smiling father says, "I just wanted the satisfaction of having my own Nintendo finger!"

For laughs, try watching a child teach a video game to a friend. First the novice watches the veteran play. Twenty-one minutes later, he finally gets his turn. His game lasts all of twenty-one seconds. The friend never says "try it again," but instead plays the game once more for twenty-one minutes. And so on and so on. Maybe this explains why every kid needs his own video game set!

We buy our kids cartridge after cartridge, even though they soon get tired of each and every one. Asked to name the hottest game, one youngster responded, "Super Mario Bros. III." What's passe? "Super Mario Bros. II." Don't even ask about I.

And Nintendo has now introduced Game Boy, a

completely separate, hand-held video game unit, which requires its *own* cartridges. Can you imagine investing in an entirely new technology while we're still paying off the old one? Congratulations, Nintendo, you know us better than we know ourselves.

And if our children aren't taken in by the video fad, the fashion fad is sure to take hold. Remember when tennis shoes were just tennis shoes? Not a statement of our style, not a reflection of our worth or athletic prowess, not an item guaranteed to make us more popular or successful on the court.

Pity the earlier generations who were so dimwitted they took their tennis shoes for granted. Some parents spend ninety dollars and more to give their children the brand that Madison Avenue says is correct. And by the time the canvas wonders have one-tenth of a mile on them, a different brand will be even hotter, and our children will be begging for those.

The shoes, unfortunately, are the tip of the iceberg. Even quiet children need to make fashion statements. Parents who have the nerve to take them to the "wrong" store (i.e., affordable) are in for a shock.

If it is not bought at Benetton, the Gap, Esprit, or one of the hundred other hot specialty stores, forget it. Buy a kid a sweater from K-Mart and the box will be opened with poorly disguised disappointment and humiliation. The garment's appearance is irrelevant;

the label is all. Wearing something ugly and hot beats pretty and Penneys anytime.

Teen magazine has actually raised the right to spend money on "name" fashion to the constitutional level. In a recent article, "Loco Over Labels—Label Yourself in Style," the editors advised our young to "practice your right to free speech by wearing your favorite trademarks, designer names, and emblems, and make their messages your personal passwords." Instead of the Bill of Rights, we now have the right to bills.

A recent report in a newspaper indicates how acceptable this mania for fashion has become. A banker was sitting at the dinner table with his two daughters, relating that he was very near to obtaining a customer's signature on a very important business deal.

His daughters started chanting, "Close, Close." Initially the banker took this as thoughtful sales encouragement, that he should "close" the deal. Instead, he quickly discovered that the girls were really chanting "Clothes, Clothes," in anticipation of additions to their wardrobe if their dad was successful.

This is a relatively innocent affair. But should one feel so proud of this reflexive, materialistic response that it winds up in the local paper?

Everybody tries to exploit the social insecurity of our growing children for their benefit. And we parents pay.

Looking to provide prepackaged formulas for

popularity, one company advertises "Teen Cards." These are informative sets which are mailed to subscribers once a month, just like a book or record club, providing tips on making friends, relationships, fashion, etc. What can these cards do for you? "Be a winner! Look better. . .Dress better. Feel better. Be more popular. . ." Of course, the ad makes no mention of grades.

In addition to providing video games and designer clothing, many of us turn our kids into world travelers, mini Marco Polos with their own luggage and kiddie Fodors. Call a child nowadays and there's at least a thirty percent chance he'll be in Europe. Many kids routinely leave the country once a year, and have a passport with more stamps than a small-town post office.

These trips begin with the obligatory sojourn to Disney World, usually undertaken when our kids are still just young enough to spoil the trip. But the Florida Peninsula is just the beginning. Recently I was having lunch with a friend of my son. To make conversation, I asked which was his favorite restaurant. He answered, "Well, there's this place in Nassau. . . ."

Kids today ski at Vail, catch the Wimbledon in London, and play basketball in Romania. Reflecting these trends, Delta Air Lines recently introduced Dusty the Delta Air Lion and Fantastic Flyer Programs for kids aged two to twelve. Coffee, tea, or crayons, anyone?

Might not traveling around one's own state or region in a plain old car be as appropriate for our young ones? And if we're planning a luxurious trip, must the kids *always* come along? Travel is truly wonderful, but isn't there some downside to providing these fantastic opportunities at such young ages?

Again, we seem hell-bent on providing our children with so many wonderful experiences that they will have nothing to look forward to once they've reached their majority.

Kids seemingly know no limits in restaurants, either. Kiddie menus apparently are no longer for kids. Why is this? The portions are right, as is the price. Obviously if we can afford it, we should expose our kids to a fancy restaurant occasionally, both to help them learn proper etiquette and to give them the thrill of a special experience. But many young ones dine on crab legs or lamb chops every week, and routinely order the most expensive thing on the menu without asking if it's okay.

Even our neighborhood ice cream stands have gone upscale. Remember the good old days, B.B. (before Blizzards)? Our children could have one scoop of ice cream and actually be satisfied. Now they require the large Blizzard at $2.25. Take four kids out for a treat, and kiss away nine bucks. Before the four large Cokes.

Many parents wouldn't begin to set a dollar limit on their kids' frozen treats. And many children would refuse to "schlep" (i.e., be driven) to the custard stand if all they could have was custard.

Smart marketers are aware of our children's acquisitive streaks, and are targeting record numbers of products at them. Colgate and Crest both offer kiddie toothpastes, with sparkles. Like all else nowadays, brushing needs to be fun.

But the product that really says it all is the Polaroid Cool Cam, a camera conceived and developed just for kids (remember when using the same camera as our folks was actually acceptable?). Polaroid interviewed hundreds of kids aged nine to fourteen and came up with the "newest instant camera for contemporary kids" (uncontemporary kids apparently weren't spoken to).

The camera is hot pink or grey, the "right" colors for the target market, and comes with color-coordinated camera case and sunglasses. Pity the unstylish geeks whose cameras don't match their shades.

The Wall Street Journal interviewed some parents and kids during a recent Christmas, and some of the opinions expressed provide insights to the best and worst that is happening.

One mom was asked what her child wanted for Christmas. She replied, "There's nothing out there he likes. He hasn't even thought about writing to Santa Claus yet." However, she went on to say that he had asked for a computer. Isn't that a sufficient wish list for a six-year-old?

And a wonderful boy of eleven probably gave us the answer to our traumas when he described the kind of Christmas he expected. The young gentleman wanted a Nintendo set, but his father wasn't going to buy it. So the kid said to the reporter, "This is going to be a $9.99 Christmas."

We will need many such gift-giving occasions before our children develop an appreciation for all that they have in this amazing land of plenty.

POINTS TO REMEMBER

- If we have skate exchanges for our kids' skates, why can't we have cartridge exchanges for their video games?

- Dollar amounts greater than ten should not be preceded by the word "only."

- Hot video games are dead within three months.

- Fast feet will lead to athletic excellence faster than hot footwear.

- When everybody buys at the same hot store, it will close within a year.

- Children should see their own state before visiting a foreign one.

- In a fancy restaurant, our kids' entrees should rarely be the table's most expensive.

- Never buy a phone whose eyes open and close.

- Despite appearances, there are more feet in this country than brands of tennis shoes.

- The more money we spend on treats for our son's friends at an ice cream stand, the less likely they will thank us.

Don't Worry, Be Happy

As WE GIVE OUR CHILDREN MORE AND MORE, we seem to be demanding and receiving less and less. Trendiness and excess are often winning the battle against respect, civility, and family unity. Cursing parents is common, displaying disrespect to grandparents routine. Academic excellence is often just for nerds, and outside jobs are for grinds and geeks.

The very children who begged us years ago for toy vacuums and play lawn mowers won't help out around the house if their lives depended on it. And on the rare occasion when they *do,* they act put upon, as if performing an immense favor, and will perform the task poorly. All the better to maintain the fiction that they are the ones to be waited on.

Despite such attitudes, we reward these kids with never-ending activities. Look at the fortune the World Wrestling Federation takes in with its various pay-per-view wrestling extravaganzas. The cost is $19.95 and up, but that doesn't faze the little Hulksters for even a three count. Perhaps they think dad is really The Million Dollar Man.

We allow perfectly wonderful outings to be destroyed by our propensity for excess. Several years ago I enrolled one of my kids in a bowling league. He loved it. But do you know what most kids did when they were there? Not bowl, but play video games. The ingrates actually had to be called out of the video game room when it was their turn.

Are all the lessons and extra activities we provide for our kids really necessary? The ballet instruction, gymnastics, basketball camp, art school, and tennis lessons don't come cheap. Do they really deserve karate lessons at forty bucks a month? That's practically five hundred dollars a year!

Children used to make plans on their own, didn't they? Home was boring, so they'd get up a neighborhood football game or a game of jump rope. Now they sit in their rooms alone, glancing idly at the TV for hours or playing video games against the computer. We've provided such entertainment palaces that they don't need to play with others.

Homework is no longer a priority to most of our children. It is an option, to be completed if they're "in the mood." As a result, our schools are being burdened with a shocking increase in incompletes and skipped assignments. The video games are more fun, and that's what life is supposed to be about. And we parents often sit by and do nothing.

Perhaps our kids' problems would be lessened if the schools stressed and rewarded true excellence. Many systems now unfortunately concentrate on rewarding children for just simply *not* misbehaving. A child often comes home with more stickers, awards, and little edible treats than the average variety store has in inventory. What did the star pupil do? Not much, just sit quietly and not disrupt.

The class trouble-maker, who disrupted just four times a week rather than twenty-five, becomes the Student of the Month. And if a child misbehaves repeatedly, administrators stress understanding for the troubled homelife rather than consequences.

Wouldn't it make sense to take proper behavior for granted, and aggressively punish poor behavior so that it won't recur?

Organizers of kiddie athletic events fall into this same trap. It is apparently against the law for a child to compete and not come home with a ribbon or trophy. Shouldn't the opportunity to play be sufficient?

I know of one kids' bowling league that had just four teams. Would you believe that at the end of the season, all four teams received trophies! And I'm sure that the kids on the last place team proudly display their "Fourth Place" trophy. This is all well and good for the trophy makers, but what is this doing to our kids?

Because our children are now programed to always expect awards, they never learn to deal with disappointment. And they frequently dream of future stardom.

I honestly believe that all the lessons, rewards for mediocrity, and expensive equipment we provide enable our children to harbor the serious illusion that they will be professional athletes when they grow up.

Everyone knows the dough *they* make, so why work in school? The kid who closed his eyes and somehow connected on the game-winning home run in his Little League game feels he's the next Jose Canseco. The eight-year-old with the unhittable ground strokes thinks of herself as the next Chris Evert.

Because they believe they know it all (they always get awards, don't they?), our little jocks aren't even willing to pay their dues and develop their skills. A volunteer basketball coach having his initial practice with a group of nine-year-olds is confronted with something like this:

"Okay, gentlemen, gather round. I'm your coach, and I'd like to introduce myself."

Instantly a hand is raised. "Coach, when is our first game?"

"I don't know yet," comes the reply. "First we've got to practice our fundamentals."

So the children shoot for three minutes. Soon the

coach confronts one particular child. "Jason, why are you trying long, three-point shots?"

"Didn't you say to practice fundamentals?" comes the reply. "By the way, do you know when our first game is?"

"No I don't, son," you shoot back. "Let's all line up for a passing drill."

After thirty seconds of hell, eight bored children simultaneously ask, "Coach, this isn't fun. Can we scrimmage against the team practicing at that other basket?"

"No way," comes your reply. "We need to develop our skills. Let's now. . ."

A child interrupts. "Coach, do you know when our first game is?"

We are raising kids who would rather show off their behind-the-back dribble than practice a boring old lay-up or a free throw. Almost none of these pretenders have the discipline required to achieve their true athletic potential.

The sportsmanship we see at athletic events is becoming poorer every season. Fights are increasingly common, from pro sports on down.

Once when one of my kids was in a basketball program for eight-year-olds, all the children on the opposing team yelled "miss" before every free throw attempt. Did the coach tell them it was wrong? When they persisted, did he tell them they'd be benched if they continued?

And at high school basketball games, students chant "bullshit" after every blown call by the referee, and yell "boring" during the presentation by the opposition's cheerleaders.

The myth of becoming a superstar athlete is so strong, I don't believe I've ever seen any statistics on the odds against it. To become a pro football player, you have to be super big, super strong, or super fast. That eliminates ninety-eight percent of our kids right there, even with steroids.

Look at pro basketball. You have to be a giant. Even the guards are often over six-four. The twenty-seven NBA teams annually draft just two players apiece.

On average, only one of them will make the team. Given that every year about a million and a half boys are born, that means the odds of making an NBA team for even a year are about 1 in 55,555. And given the chance of injuries and being released, the odds of becoming a superstar are infinitesimal.

Through some quirk of fate (call it the Bosworth Bias), the pro athlete our kids most idolize is the last one we would want for such an important role. Who have been the hot ones? Brian Bosworth, Jim McMahon, John McEnroe. Outrageous is in; civility is out.

Big companies, like Gillette, Taco Bell, and Bic lighters, have even used these "role models" to move their products.

But the classic way to show the importance of sports to kids is the marketing miracle of Gatorade. Have you tasted the stuff? Try it sometime, and see if you can imagine your kids enjoying it. Yet because they think the pros drink it, it is popular. The ad claims it restores fluids to the body. Quite a trick for a beverage, huh?

We parents further this youthful obsession with sports by going to all the games. It is now our job to attend every inning, chucker, period, quarter, and half of our children's athletic endeavors (regardless of the weather).

And the different teams encourage attendance, even making us feel guilty if we aren't there to "support" our youngsters. Most of our folks never came to watch *us* when we played on the playground. Why must it be different today? Isn't it possible that we make these events seem too important by *always* attending?

I know one couple that actually brags about its efforts every weekend to watch the soccer games of *each* of their four kids. Saturday *and* Sunday are sometimes allocated to this important purpose. Why not watch just one game each weekend? These folks work all week. Aren't the weary entitled to some time for themselves?

With all the entertainment and sports opportunities, kids seemingly have no time left for earning money. Adults increasingly are the ones delivering our newspapers, as this time-honored method of teaching the value of money is perceived by kids as a waste of time.

Has a child knocked on your door in the last year offering any services? They're not out on my block.

And if we force our children to try to get jobs, they know how to play the game. They won't take the initiative, but may allow their name to be put on the list of neighborhood helpers circulated by the middle school.

However, when anyone calls looking for a worker, they'll have an excuse. "I have a big exam tomorrow" (so get up earlier), "Sorry, I'm sleeping over at a friend's house" (so change your plans for ten bucks an hour), etc., etc.

We parents are far from faultless in all this. We do too much for our kids. We buy them too much, and give them too much spending money. Otherwise they would work.

And we don't allow them to walk. If it's raining we drive them home from school, even though they will continue to play for hours if it is raining during their Little League game. Many children call their folks for rides although they are only four or five blocks from home. In safe neighborhoods, in broad daylight.

We never force our kids to make choices. Two siblings want to see different TV shows at the same time? No problem! They each watch in separate bedrooms.

And if they can't decide which program to view, don't worry, some newer sets show two channels simultaneously!

Rather than forcing them to choose, we allow our children to play both baseball and soccer, and stand ready to whisk them from one to the other so they can enjoy both, regardless of the inconvenience to us.

If we needed proof that something is horribly wrong with the kids we are raising, consider this. A recent study in Rhode Island asked 1,700 seventh through ninth graders their attitudes on rape. On the question of whether it was okay for a boy to *force* a girl to kiss him after a date, fifty-one percent of the boys and forty-one percent of the girls said it was fine.

But it gets far worse. When asked if it's okay for a boy to *force* a girl to have sex after spending a lot of money on her (ten to fifteen dollars), twenty-four percent of the boys and sixteen percent of the girls agreed.

Now here is the killer. When asked whether it was okay for a boy to *force* a girl to have sex with him if they had been dating for six months, sixty-five percent of the boys said it was okay, and an astonishing forty-seven percent of the girls agreed. Are we becoming lost as a society or what?

If we really want to see what our kids value, try to get them to sell a "hot" ticket they possess to a sold-out New Kids concert. Forget offering face value;

that would be an insult. Some kids wouldn't sell their thirty-dollar tickets for a hundred, two hundred, or even a thousand dollars. Try this out. The results are truly saddening.

A midwestern rabbi perhaps best summarized what kids are looking for today. It seems that some children walked out of a religious service they were invited to and instead roamed the temple and caused some damage. As the rabbi said, we have taught our children that "this whole society exists for their pleasure, and if a particular given moment isn't fun, then they've got to make it fun."

In the home, school, and practically everywhere, this generation needs to have its "fun." And we parents, society, and our kids themselves are paying a high price indeed.

POINTS TO REMEMBER

- Only ineffective parents get sworn at by their children.

- Parents who don't insist that their children help with chores have no right to complain about being treated like butlers and maids.

- Children should occasionally consider participating in sports activities that parents don't pay for.

- If our children don't regularly turn in their homework, our discipline is also incomplete.

- Rewarding mediocrity is the surest way to aid society's decline.

- The best parents don't need to watch every single sporting event their children take part in.

- If we don't require our children to do odd jobs, we shouldn't complain about the decline of the work ethic.

- Walking is healthier for our children than driving in the car.

- True fun can occur only when it is the exception and not the rule.

- Practicing a sport will enhance one's skills more than watching on TV.

- Parents who allow the TV to be on during dinner should admit they have no interest in communicating with their children.

- An injury will hurt a sliding Little Leaguer more if he is called "out" rather than "safe."

- Souvenirs bought at a rock concert should not exceed the cost of the ticket by a ratio of more than 4-1.

High School Horrors

*D*URING THE HIGH SCHOOL YEARS, THE habits in the making since birth are refined and accelerate. Possessions increase, and appearances decline. Respect for others often disappears altogether. Shoplifting is "neat," an acceptable shortcut to that which our kids feel they are so clearly entitled.

It is but a short step from video games to MTV, CD players, stereos, and cable. Even though they only go places in cars, every teenager needs a "Walkman."

Can anyone remember when a CD was a savings certificate? Now compact disc players are the rage. All of the old record players (excuse me, stereo systems) are now worthless, replaced by a new technology with better sound.

Remember listening to records when we were kids? Was the sound inferior? How'd we get by in those dark ages? Although we allow our kids to step up their technology on demand, like complete fools we con-

SPOILED ROTTEN . . .

tinue to use our old car or ancient mower. After all, why throw something out if it still works?

Kids' rooms often contain more electronics than small FM stations. TVs, stereos, CD players, boom boxes, Walkmen, and cordless phones, not to mention the four-head VCRs (two heads are only good enough for parents). It's amazing there's still room for the water-bed and the poster of the rock star who uses drugs.

Listen to two kids argue about whose systems are better and you're in for a real treat:

"What do you mean your stereo is nicer? My speakers are bigger than yours!"

"Yeah," the other one replies, "but my boom box has Dolby, and my Walkman has padded earcups."

"Big deal," comes the retort. "Your VCR only has two heads, and you can't even program it by phone."

"Granted," the other concedes, "but my answering machine has a beeperless remote."

From here the conversation goes downhill (if that's possible), resulting in a zesty crossfire of swear words and other graphic equalizers.

Remember when the first question children asked when moving into a new apartment was whether it had a swimming pool? Now they ask if it's wired for cable. Despite all the free TV we bring into the home over our six sets, we must invest twenty to forty dollars a month to bring in such "quality" programing as MTV.

Have you ever sat down and actually watched the music videos we pay for? The American Academy of Pediatricians, not the least respected organization in our country, recently warned parents about them, suggesting that they glorify and promote violence.

Watch the things sometime. One video has a beautiful woman on her hands and knees, depicted as an animal in a ring surrounded by leering, screaming men. In the words of one pediatrician, "MTV won't air public service announcements about abstinence or ads for birth control, yet is filled with half-dressed women serving as empty-headed playthings for males."

And yet we pay to provide this entertainment for our kids. If our children claim a free speech right to watch this kind of programing, we should claim the free market right of having them help pay. And it will get worse.

A new company is developing technology so that kids can dial a number and a specific video will appear on their TV. Only two bucks a shot. Guess who's going to wind up paying for this new marvel?

Many parents reward their sixteen-year-olds with their own cars, even though the kids haven't given them a decent day since they rode their scooters. Air conditioning is an essential (even if our car doesn't have it), as is the deluxe stereo system.

And our children often contribute nothing to the

cost of any of this: not for the car, the gas, the insurance, speeding tickets, or even the repairs.

Many kids today live at shopping malls, those marvelous collections of upscale retail shops which have helped make the phrase "shop till you drop" the new American anthem. Ask them what they do there, and you'll hear that they "hang out." And because we're really scared to know the truth, we let the subject drop.

Confronting a child with complaints about his time spent at malls usually provides no satisfaction:

"Josh, you have to get cracking at school. You haven't gone near a book in the past three weeks."

"That's not true, dad," he replies. "I walk past the Walden Books every day."

"Good try, but that doesn't count. I will not tolerate these mediocre grades."

"What's wrong with being average?" he retorts. "Lincoln was no scholar, and Einstein flunked kindergarten."

Isn't it absolutely amazing how teens who never read their history books can recall the names of all famous people who received poor grades?

"Those successes were atypical," you argue. "Their luck may not come your way."

"But my favorite FM disc jockey says that many people are late bloomers, especially Leos."

"If I've told you once, I've told you a thousand

times. I refuse to have a discussion with a young man who uses as an authority a person who referees belching contests. Now this must end."

But of course it doesn't.

Kids who get thrown out of malls gravitate to fast food restaurants. If you've ever sat next to such a group, you know that the scene is not especially pretty.

Modern teen etiquette seems to require an average of three loud belches per booth occupant. Just as at home, the kids often leave the table a mess, and treat the "help" with disrespect.

Schools seem powerless to change the situation. Have you noticed how kids go to school nowadays? Filthy and torn blue jeans apparently further the educational process. And how can schools allow sweatshirts with beer logos?

And if our children wear the wrong color baseball cap, or a piece of hot clothing, they risk being mugged, or worse. The jeans are tight, the blouses are revealing, and the hormones are out of control.

Teen sex is a rite of passage, free of commitment and obligation. The love our daughter rejects from us she often tries to get from others. And we're supposed to sit back and watch, with a broken heart, as if we don't know what's happening.

As the poster for the Children's Defense Fund asks, "Will your child learn to multiply before she learns to subtract?"

A recent article on high school sex highlights the extent of the gratification the current generation requires. A sixteen-year-old boy was asked why he never used condoms. His reply, "It feels better without them." So much for fear of fatherhood!

Grades of course are continually declining across the country. In some cities, up to one-third of high schoolers are *habitually* truant. Homework is for geeks; fun is for everyone else. Many children graduate high school without knowing how to read or write effectively. Seniors can't tell you which sides fought the Civil War, or find France (or even Arkansas) on a map.

During one of these "lack of knowledge" surveys, one girl actually identified Chernoble, the site of the Soviet nuclear power accident, as Cher's family name. Isn't it time we made national educational standards a reality? And shouldn't we be denying driver's licenses to competent students who can't meet them?

But woe upon the individual who tries to increase standards. Teachers who require excellence, and therefore give out too many low grades, are immediately told by parents, principals, and School Board members to knock it off. No one asks to look at the actual exams in question, to see if a reasonably serious student might have done well. The simple fact that so many kids did poorly indicts the test.

As in our day, the football star is the hero, rotten

personality and all. And the gym is bedecked with special plaques commemorating outstanding athletic feats. The fastest time in school history for each track and swimming event is proudly recorded for posterity, a goal for today's athletes to shoot for. But nowhere are the names displayed of those who earned four-point averages, or wrote perfect SATs.

Recently, I was surprised to find *color* pictures in the Chicago Tribune of some of the students selected as all-state athletes in volleyball and soccer. I'll bet the Tribune has rarely run a color picture of a teenager who wasn't an athlete. Enter college at eleven, save six kids from a burning building, do thousands of hours of volunteer work, and black and white is good enough. But spike well, and the sky's the limit.

Although their grades are often mediocre, many teens aren't required to hold a job, even during the summer.

And for those who do work, the money they earn often is spent on clothes or videos rather than their continuing education. Many teen workers will call in sick rather than miss the hot party. And it is not a good omen that employers increasingly put up signs that read, "*Good* Help Wanted."

Our inability to require excellence does little to prepare our kids for life. While children in other countries have a longer school year and concentrate on demanding studies, many of our kids are listening to their boom boxes, watching TV, or cruising malls. And when it finally comes time to compete against their peers in foreign nations, is anyone really surprised by the outcome?

POINTS TO REMEMBER

- Our children's TVs should not be bigger and better than ours.

- If you have a disrespectful child, don't buy her a car when she's sixteen. One lemon at a time is great plenty.

- Kids used to have more time than money. Now the reverse is true.

- Table manners of teenagers fortunately improve with age.

- Teenage boys who risk a girl becoming pregnant are not men.

- Most teachers who demand uncompromising excellence will leave the field in frustration.

- An athlete will be excused for any offense except disloyalty to his team.

- The last lawn mower a teenager walked behind should not have been giving off bubbles.

Fun on Campus

ALONG ABOUT THE MIDDLE OF THEIR JUNIOR year in high school, many of our best and brightest come down with "future shock," and finally realize that if they don't want to become a normal, working member of society they had better start thinking about college.

Even though we've been encouraging and cajoling excellence since kindergarten, *now* is when it dawns on them. Where we failed, the threat of an impending job succeeds.

The outbreak of studying that occurs is both wondrous and saddening to the unbelieving, shell-shocked parent. While gratified to see the newly inspired scholars capable of such effort, we're irritated that they bypassed so many earlier educational opportunities. Nonetheless, studying is studying.

Remember when deciding on a college *didn't* drive

a family crazy? Or the good old days when a four-year education didn't cost more than a home?

High schoolers begin their search by sending away for catalogs from every institution they've ever heard of. Our kids are not especially selective—they'll assume we'll be willing to pay the tuition, regardless how high.

Several rules of thumb seem to apply when children get serious about selecting sites for further education. First, they only choose schools more expensive than their parents can afford. Second, they only apply to institutions that their grades won't allow them to enter. "If only I could take my freshman, sophomore, and half my junior year over," they say to themselves. "Then I'd show them." And lastly, the public institution in the neighboring state is always preferable to the one in their own.

As our children consider sending off applications to half the schools in the nation, they develop academic interests we were never aware of.

The teen who twice sent his younger brother to the hospital in domestic squabbles announces that he wants to work with children. The daughter who takes a week to read a Golden Book is now a future librarian. And they select colleges on this basis, even though they'll change their major three times during the freshman orientation.

Recent studies show that one of three American

divorces are caused by the notorious "essays" required on college admissions forms. Some families spend more time plotting "strategy" than they've spent together in the last four years. Inevitably mom and dad can't agree on the proper answers, so for once the child tries to be a diplomat.

Kids and their parents become fiction writers. The child who's never read a newspaper claims an intense interest in world affairs. A latent crusader whose favorite phrase is "Shit Happens" writes about his optimistic twelve-point program to improve the world. And the admissions officers allow this hoax to go merrily along—they're getting their application fees, aren't they?

Many children need to visit their target colleges, every single one of them, to get a "feel" for the campus. Mom and dad take off from their jobs, and arrange a hectic tour of America's leading schools. The cost is irrelevant. Often the kids wind up at the state university anyway, or make snap judgements based on irrelevant experiences. It rained on the day they showed up in New Haven? Scratch Yale. The dorms are too small at UCLA? Forget it! The tour guide at the University of Michigan had acne? Gross!

Once admitted to various schools, our children now drive us crazy with their indecisiveness. A week from the deadline, our talks with them usually go like this:

"How are you leaning today, dear?" you inquire.

"Well, Andrea is heading to Duke if her boyfriend gets in, and Roger is holding off between Indiana and Purdue to see who signs the high school sports phenom. So I just don't know."

"Isn't it about time to be making a final decision?" you gently ask.

"Oh, I will, mom. I just need more time," comes the reply. "Did you see Wisconsin got eight inches of snow last week? I don't have a decent pair of boots."

"I know it's complex, dear," you answer, "but we just want you to be happy."

And so it goes until the coin flip, which allows a final decision to be made and a future to be sewn.

Unlimited money now flows to our collegians for living expenses, and mom and dad never ask for an accounting. Shame on us. But there are some advantages. Where would you list marijuana on a balance sheet? And if the students run short of funds, there's always the Mastercharge. What's a little interest between friends?

Phone calls home sometimes express interest in money but not grandma. And although students complain about tuition increases, somehow they manage to attend every important rock concert. Rather than spending vacations at home, getting reacquainted with the family, or God forbid working, they can be found on the slopes at Vail or on the beach at Cancun.

And throughout their four years of college, they will often forget to say thank you.

Students discover many academic shortcuts along the way. Many join fraternities and find access to exam files. Or take easy courses. Do you know that at the University of Illinois, you can get credit for pocket billiards and the anthropology of play? Or consider the University of Massachusetts, which offers credit for slimnastics and frisbee. But if you like rock music, consider Cal State, L.A. Don't miss Music Video 454. Really.

Believe it or not, two national organizations actually advertise term papers for sale. Research Assistance has a three hundred and six-page catalog with detailed descriptions of 16,278 research papers ready for your use, "a virtual library of information at your fingertips." Cost is "just" seven bucks a page, with a maximum fee of a hundred and nineteen dollars. But don't fret, folks, the footnote and bibliography pages are free.

If you require "custom" research, this organization claims to have a staff of "seventy-five professional writers, each writing in his field of expertise. . . ." And there's a toll-free 800-number for ordering (on dad's charge card, no doubt).

Another outfit, Berkeley Research, offers the same service. Just reach for a credit card, and your scholarly worries are over. Parents will take great solace in learning that at least there's competition in this unusual marketplace, as Berkeley invites users to "compare our prices."

Can you imagine spending fifteen thousand dollars a year on tuition and having a student *buy* a term paper? After all, Research Assistance "has been serving the national academic community since October, 1969." How can national publications provide these services a forum?

Soon attending classes won't even be necessary. On most major campuses, some of the better students are hired to sit in on classes and take notes for a note-taking service. Or a professor voluntarily makes available all her lecture notes.

At one school, a kid spent twenty-one dollars on notes from forty-eight biology lectures, and received a B instead of a possible F. And he didn't even step into the lecture hall, except for the exam.

Soon, kids will be bragging that they earned a college degree and never entered a classroom. That the schools don't put a stop to this nonsense is crazy.

Even apolitical college students believe in the two party system—one on Friday night, and another on Saturday night. Actually, it's only a boring campus that gets excited about two parties a week; for some kids, the entire college experience is one big party.

Drinking has reached epidemic proportions on all our college campuses. The bar is where the action is, not the library. Students imbibe drink after drink, in a desperate attempt to appear happy. Puking is how they know it is almost time to stop.

Recently Boston's Licensing Board passed an ordinance banning alcohol at parties in student housing. Said the Board's chairwoman, "It's a sad commentary . . . but keg parties have become the only form of student activism. . . ." Local liquor stores are banned from delivering kegs and cases of beer to colleges. Underscoring the necessity for such a measure, one Northeastern University student commented, "You come to college to learn and drink. They can't stop it."

Alcoholic outrages occur on all our campuses. At Kent State University, the hockey program was suspended after freshman players were forced to drink excessively, resulting in one being hospitalized for three days. The same kind of thing occurs at Princeton on down. Every year we hear of fraternity pledges dying from an "innocent" alcoholic initiation rite.

And if the drinking isn't taking time away from the studies, the sex is. The term "big man on campus" suddenly has new meaning. Student dormitories are now co-ed, with the right to have overnight guests emblazoned in stone. Often our daughters have to share a dorm room with their roommate *and* the roommate's boyfriend.

Fraternities of course cause troubles of their own.

For many kids they are indispensable, the prime social unit of their college years. Graduates recall them fondly, but the excesses along the way are all too plentiful. Most of the racial and ethnic incidents seem to involve fraternities in one way or another. The drinking is legendary, and the convenient beds a source of "happy" males and pregnant coeds.

At Florida State University, a fraternity was banned for five years for the alleged rape of a teenage student. At the University of Michigan, some pantyraiders entered dorm rooms unannounced and asked for panties and autographs on their naked posteriors.

At Texas Christian University, girls who are accepted into sororities have to run a gauntlet of two hundred men, who can touch them anywhere they please. Says one coed: "It was awful. They grabbed you everywhere and anywhere they could reach. But it was fun. It's something everybody has to do." Why do the men take part? As a Sigma Chi says, "Tradition, bud, tradition."

Date rape is all over our campuses. It is growing daily, and as one counselor has said, for many kids "is a way of life." A 1985 survey of thirty-two campuses reported that one in eight coeds said they had been forced to have sex. And the figures are growing every day. I guess the boys we have managed to raise are used to getting *everything* they want.

Of course, many students do find time to study

long and hard despite these diversions. But even so, triviality still reigns. The campus practically shuts down during its favorite soap. And if Michael Jordan and the President of the United States showed up simultaneously, we know who'd spark the greater interest.

Mike Royko, syndicated columnist for the Chicago Tribune, recently had a great idea. He argued that the term teenager covers too many years, that the difference between an insecure young boy of thirteen and a strong, confident nineteen-year-old man of the world is immense. He's right. We keep our kids juveniles so long it's a wonder that they ever grow up.

After college, many of our kids defer marriage for ten to twenty years, as if that guarantees a happy union. Marriages no longer occur six months after love blooms, but instead take place when the couple has enough cash for a good-sized home with quality furniture. Gone are the struggling years, which couples previously looked back upon as among their happiest.

But generally the kids do marry, and as these things go, wind up producing children, children destined to have it better than they. And the cycle of spoiling starts all over again.

POINTS TO REMEMBER

- A student can select a college without visiting it.

- This is not the first generation to discover that partying is more fun than work.

- The number of colleges a child applies to should not exceed twice his high school grade point average.

- Students who drink the most are the least happy.

- Most successful con men get their starts answering essay questions on college application forms.

- Collegians who don't thank relatives for gifts don't deserve any.

- A fun-filled college experience isn't of value if by graduation the students can't spell "party."

- It's hard for students to claim they can't afford a tuition increase if they regularly visit a tanning booth.

CHANGING
OUR KIDS

Disorder All Over

*T*HE SPOILING OF OUR CHILDREN AND THE undesirable behavior which results coincide with other trends that are affecting the quality of our life. The problems didn't start with our kids, and they won't end with them. They are a symptom of something very wrong in our land, of an America gone dramatically astray.

The more economic progress we enjoy, the larger our problems seem to be. Perhaps this is inevitable, and preferable to severe economic stagnation.

But now we seem to have a depression of the spirit rather than of the economy. People spend two thousand dollars on a sweater, and twelve hundred on shoes. We can afford great estates, but home security systems are a requirement. Even people who put in sixteen hour days need pills to fall asleep. In a land dedicated to optimism and rational thought, alcohol and drugs poison our minds and destroy us by the millions.

We've become a society of fads, with few values that are permanent. Sushi today, kiwi tomorrow. The in-spot we danced at last month is closed by year end. And we don't care. We used to require at least some clear value for our money. No longer. We know our fads are short-lived, and it doesn't matter.

Our career planning consists of deciding which state's lottery we will win. The first place prize in the Publishers Clearing House sweepstakes is a staggering *ten* million—five million is no longer a motivator.

The word "hot" has developed a cache all its own, the litmus test of what is sought after. If something is hot, it must be purchased. If the right magazine says it's hot, buy it! The media, the manufacturers, and the publicity agents combine to convince us of an item's soaring marketing momentum. And like sheep we often respond.

Remember the pandemonium several years back when Michael Jackson peaked? This was not just the normal adulation offered a star by his fans, but almost a messianic transfer of love and affection to another. We were practically deifying him. And when the hype was over, Michael came back down to earth. A great performer, but no longer a God. For we quickly go on to worship another.

Tracking all the recent fads would be a yeoman job. Don Johnson wears a pony tail—change your hair style at once. Mexican food is taking off—pass me a tortilla. The glamorous people drink bottled water—bottoms up. It doesn't really matter what our opinion is, it's what we think the crowd is doing.

We are a society in a hurry. Our restaurants are drive-thru, our planes supersonic, our screwdrivers power driven, and our eyeglasses and photographs are developed in about an hour. Even our murders are drive-by. We spend fortunes on quick weight loss schemes and get-rich-quick quackery. And we force ourselves to live at this pace, always hustling, always moving, perhaps so we never have to stop and reflect upon our relationships and our lives.

The problems confronting us are enormous, familiar to us all. Divorces and child abuse are epidemic. Alcohol and drug abuse result in immeasurable misery and death. Forty-six million of us take sleeping pills at night, and five million are insomniacs. At any one time, fully fifteen percent of us are suffering mental disorders. Crime, pornography, and sexual assaults are all soaring, with no end in sight.

Walk into a bookstore, and you will find something new. In addition to sections with books on "Travel" and "History," there are now sections called "Dependency and Recovery." Does that say a lot or what?

The specific picture of our kids is no better. Teen pregnancy is a nationwide epidemic, as are sexual diseases. Drinking and drug abuse are accepted indulgences from rural Maine to mid-L.A. A million students annually drop out of our high schools, and random murders, rapes, cults, and horrible tales of the occult occur with increasing frequency.

Our schools sometimes barely function. Teachers are often sworn at and assaulted, and metal detectors scan students for knives and worse. Our graduates often lack the writing and reading skills requisite for a modestly hopeful future.

The heroes of our kids provide precious little inspiration. Each day we learn of a new rock star obtaining a divorce, having another child out of wedlock, beating a mate, or checking into a treatment center. A young singer can't even dream of being a big star without bashing a few cameramen over the head. And the media report these behaviors with glamor and pizazz.

Can't we take some steps against these folks? Would it be so bad if the FCC mandated that songs by convicted drug users couldn't be played on the radio for six months? If these multi-millionaires claim they now can't earn money, tough, they should have considered that previously. Couldn't Hollywood dictate that child stars who enter treatment centers by age fourteen can't appear in a movie again till age eighteen? Sure, the attorneys will have a field day, but don't we have to do *something?*

Athletics particularly is out of control. Sports occupies a divine, almost holy place for us. We glorify

the athlete, and pay him a fortune. And the impact
of money is everywhere. Now it is the Mazda Gator
Bowl, the Mobil Cotton Bowl, and the Federal Express
Orange Bowl. Can it be long till we have the Sony
Olympics?

It's hard to believe that our love affair with sports
hasn't always been so intense. Again, a lot of
the blame goes to our good friend, television. The
Heisman Trophy used to be just a trophy for the year's
best college football player, not a shrine awarded
on a national telecast. As Paul Hornung, a former
Heisman winner, recently said, the trophy didn't have
"one one-hundredth" the hype back then as it does
now.

Sports are everywhere—on ESPN, all the networks,
and most places in-between. Look at the fortune
spent on the telecasts of the Olympics. NBC recently
paid $401 million for the rights to the 1992 summer
games. As recently as 1972, the same rights sold for
just $7.5 million; in 1960, $394,000. And believe it
or not, the 1960 winter games in Squaw Valley com-
manded just $50,000. Really.

Remember when the Mets came into the National
League back in 1962? Know what the franchise fee
was for the New York market? Just $1.8 million. How
our priorities have changed.

Today, even the announcers earn fortunes. The
announcers! Pat Summerall and John Madden each

command $1.7 million per year! And they have four-year contracts.

Money is affecting our sports, as it is everything. Now an appearance in a Bowl Game nets schools three million dollars. Numerous baseball players earn over two million per year. Think of it, in one year to earn so much money, for swinging a bat. That's over five thousand dollars every calendar *day* of the year, or about $1,300 per inning over a normal schedule.

If the batter comes to the plate 500 times throughout the course of the season, that's four thousand dollars *each time.* Even if he goes 0 for 4.

Clearly, these are highly talented players, and it is only fair for the owners to share the wealth with them. But given their salaries, can't we expect these athletes to be exemplary? Why don't the officials of the leagues impose strong standards on these superstars?

Everyone knows that some drug use exists in all the professional leagues. The leaders could say, "use cocaine and you're history," but they don't.

What do you think the penalty should be for a million dollar athlete using cocaine in the NFL? A year out of the league? Two years? Five years? Permanent banishment? In recent years the penalty for a *second* offense was only thirty days suspension. Are these people serious? That's an example for our kids?

And what about the thousands of people who buy expensive tickets to see drug-addicted performances? Don't drugs pose a threat to the integrity of the game? Might not a player consider underperforming on the field if a supplier threatened to make public his drug use?

Sometimes the *very* player suspended for using drugs is active in his team's "Say No To Drugs" program. The Pittsburgh Steelers actually had discussions with a potential quarterback four days after his release for three attempts to deliver cocaine. Is it any wonder that the Chairman of the U.S. Select Committee on Narcotics and Substance Abuse called for all major professional sports leagues to permanently ban players for first-time illegal drug use?

With all the money in college sports, and the win-at-all-costs mentality, college recruiting is an absolute scandal. Players get money and even girls under the table. The national joke that Southern Methodist University has the best players money can buy is not particularly funny. High school phenoms are wooed in a disgraceful display of our society's priorities. Boosters offer cash, schools offer easy courses, and the coaches actually claim they are unaware of these shenanigans.

And the pressure on kids is enormous. Recently, an Indiana high school star decided to take his basketball talents to an out-of-state school rather than the

University of Indiana. Many Hoosiers were very upset with this decision. As the player's father suggested, would they have been upset if his son was an engineer and enrolled at MIT?

When a college program is disciplined by the meek NCAA, the coach gets to stay right where he is. Wouldn't it be nice if the person with ultimate responsibility lost his job? As the Tulsa Tribune recently editorialized after Oklahoma's football team was suspended, "How many violations would occur if head coaches understood that sanctions would be followed with a request for their resignation?"

Even the Olympics is being diseased by the presence of money. Many countries pay their athletes for performance, with a going rate for gold, silver, and bronze medals. And even for American athletes, can anyone say for sure that an individual is motivated by excellence and love of country, and not by the possible Ice Capades contract and endorsement opportunities?

All these trends impact our kids on the high school and grade school level. Whenever we hear a professional star talk about a former coach, he praises him. But as the bucks become bigger, and the winner-take-all attitude of the colleges invades our high schools and grade schools, some of our kids pay a high price indeed.

Steroids are a problem even at the high school level.

If your child wrestles or plays football, talk to him. If he says no one on the team uses steroids, he is probably lying. Even *female* athletes use them. And who cares enough to contact the coach, and the School Board, to make sure policies are in place to protect our children from themselves?

And what about all the Little Leaguers ruining their arms by throwing curve balls at age twelve or thirteen. The coaches all claim innocence, and say that the pitches curve "naturally." Anyone want to buy a bridge?

Our mini-athletes mirror the obnoxious behavior they see every time they turn on the tube. Egos have never been bigger, as each player believes he's a future star. And if the coach doesn't like the player's attitude, no problem. The kid just transfers to a different high school, whose coach gladly receives him.

The disorder in our society doesn't excuse our kids' behavior, but it does help explain it:

If we chase fad after fad, why would our kids have values that are permanent?

If our children see that our success hasn't brought happiness, why would they want to achieve?

If our kids see their heroes going essentially unpunished for drug use, why would they not expect similar treatment?

And if society believes a team can win at any cost, why would children care how the game is played?

Amidst this chaos it *is* possible to effectively discipline, but the task is made more difficult. The values we demonstrate in living our own lives must be identical to those we ask of our children. For whatever their flaws, this new generation isn't dumb, and they can spot a hypocrite three miles away.

POINTS TO REMEMBER

- "Hot" is a four-letter word.

- The more lottery tickets we buy, the more money we will lose.

- Children who worship rock stars as true Gods demonstrate that they are in need of one.

- Heroes who break the law aren't worth supporting.

- College coaches should not earn more than four times the annual salary of the university president.

- A superstar athlete earning four million dollars a year should not receive a bonus for making the All-Star team.

- Parents who claim to have more than three close friends usually haven't any.

- Parents who attempt to turn their children into clones often have an unrealistic self-image.

Child Dominated Homes

REMEMBER THE GOOD OLD DAYS WHEN children were heard but not seen? Now they're often heard *and* obscene.

Foul-mouthed seven-year-olds now curse their parents, and we often stand and take it. We have placed our kids on pedestals, and our home-life revolves around them. Their every wish, thought, and feeling is a concern, till literally we're obsessed with their happiness.

Husbands and wives are second-class citizens, entitled only to the emotional leftovers. We try to make our kids' lives perfect, free from pain, as if this is desirable and achievable.

Remember what it was like when our newborn developed hiccups for the first time? We nervously watched the child shake with each one, fearing these routine contractions were portents of medical doom. In a short time the hiccups would invariably pass, and by our second child, we didn't even bother to pay attention. This is the kind of unnecessary concern we display toward our children's emotions for an entire lifetime.

We never claimed life was pain free, so why does every one of our children's minor pains tear us up?

We fret over every minute parenting decision, worried that one wrong action will cause a lifetime of grief and hardship. To breast feed or not? To continue the bottle or move to the cup? To toilet train this week or next? Why isn't Susie crawling? Amy's daughter is. What if Donna doesn't get into the best nursery school?

We all suffered countless minor heartaches and disappointments when we were growing up, but we lived to tell the tale. We probably even learned from these experiences. But we insist on denying our children that same opportunity.

Might this to some degree help explain the rise in teen suicide? Every year we hear about the A student who shoots himself after the failed exam. Or the teen who ends his life because of a failed relationship. We try to shield our children from so much pain that they never get the chance to develop skills in handling it.

We analyze and analyze. And if we ever do elect to discipline, we're required to *explain* everything to the child, to tell him how sorry we are for our actions, and to assure him of our ongoing love (as if that ever was in doubt).

We want his life, as well as shampoo, to have "no more tears." If he doesn't make the team, we say the coach is "unfair." If he doesn't get the A, his teacher is "weird." If he gets teased, we act as if it's a national tragedy. We try not to allow tantrums to last too long.

Every day needs to be pleasant, even though it's only by having rainy ones that we learn to appreciate the sunshine.

Parents make sacrifice after sacrifice, too many for our children's good. Dad works extra hours so Mary can get the doll advertised on TV, the one she'll enjoy for three weeks (if we're lucky). Mom and dad cancel that short vacation they'd planned so Brian, who hasn't given them a decent day in the last three years, can have the Christmas he deserves. And when it comes to colleges, we parents defer years of pleasure so our children can party and perhaps drop out of the school of their choice.

Boredom is something we no longer allow our children to experience. We buy them TVs, video games, and almost everything they want, just to keep them happy, as if possessions somehow lead to happiness.

Remember when children actually went outside to play? That's right, outside, with kids from the neighborhood. Now they escape into the entertainment palaces we call bedrooms, or take part in paid, supervised activities we need to arrange for them.

Did we have this many activities when we were

young? We filled our time, didn't we? Weren't we in better emotional shape than the kids of today, even though we had far less?

We shield them from work, while still claiming a belief in the work ethic. Many children have no chores at all to do around the house, and if they do, no penalty is imposed if they fail to do them. Allowances are rarely taken away, as children increasingly view spending money as an entitlement.

The camp they go to may have a program allowing campers to sell candy to defray the cost, but how many of us require participation? If they're unwilling to work a little bit, do they deserve to go to camp?

Many children literally set the tone for the homes they live in. Their opinion is the one that counts, their thoughts the ones that are catered to. When the telemarketer calls and asks to speak with the "head of the household," many honest parents would have to hand the phone to their children.

The nine-year-old doesn't feel like going bowling, so the family doesn't, even though dad is in the middle of a hot streak and would love to. Dinner is scheduled not for dad or mom's convenience, but around Erica's TV schedule. The family vacation is scheduled around the soccer tournament, and not mom or dad's calendar. Our children determine the restaurant and movie we go to, as if our opinions and preferences are worthless.

The question isn't what's good for the family, but what's good for Julie. In millions of American homes, children are in control, receiving the same kind of fawning, preferential treatment formerly reserved for elderly parents who might have lived with us.

We actually *consult* with our kids, as if they are equals. If we want to go to grandma's, and they don't, we waste our time explaining the reasons for the visit. Why not just order them to the car? Or if Joey doesn't want to wear a new sweater from his aunt, we negotiate, hoping he'll not cause a family scene by refusing to wear it. Why do we dignify our kids with reasoning powers beyond their years?

Does all our catering seem to be working? Weren't the little ones more stable when they were seen and not heard? When parents didn't have to watch them play? When they weren't treated like equals? When *we* decided which TV show the family watched?

Children who have been treated like the center of the universe can't get along with other children, and worse, sometimes even themselves. And disciplining them is a difficult challenge indeed.

POINTS TO REMEMBER

- Children belong on pedals, not pedestals.

- Kids' activities should be at the convenience of the parents, and not vice versa.

- Always arranging activities for our children will ensure their boredom when no outing is planned.

- If our kids can survive a fall from the top of a jungle gym, they'll survive our occasional wrong decision.

- If we survived our parents, our kids will probably survive us.

- Unrealistic and excessive praise of our children's skills will produce mediocre performers.

- Life has never been pain free. Our kids must experience disappointments to develop skills in handling failure and imperfection.

- There are no perfect parents.

- Giving our children honest feedback is more beneficial than excessive praise.

Punish Me Not

*I*N ONE OF THE BEACH BOYS' MOST FAMOUS songs, a female motorist has "fun, fun, fun till her daddy takes the T-Bird away."

If we were to update that song to reflect discipline in America today, the girl would still be driving, cruising the freeway without a care in the world. Her father still opposes her behavior, but instead of taking away the car, he keeps giving her ineffective warnings. For the old man now isn't tough enough to maintain the standards he claims to hold. He'd rather be liked by his daughter, and pray for her safety, than do what's right.

We have become a society of second, third, and even fourth chances. Children can misbehave with impunity, knowing that initial deviations are met with barely raised eyebrows rather than swift consequences. We've become paralyzed at the prospect of holding our kids accountable for their actions, regardless of how clearly we enunciate our standards.

What keeps us from imposing punishment? We claim to be strong supporters of society's norms, but this must not be the case. A person can rob and beat a senior citizen, and we become more concerned with rehabilitating the accused than with preventing similar assaults on innocent victims. Despite all the logic, we continue to feel for the criminal rather than the victim.

This misguided sentiment reflects more than just wanting to be liked, I think. We hold these views even when we don't know the wrongdoer. Is it just rooting for the underdog? Why is the criminal more deserving of our sympathy than the defenseless grandma? Yet we shrink from giving lengthy jail terms to convicted criminals, even though we oppose crime.

Isn't it strange? Perhaps we believe the criminal grew up in a bad environment, and isn't fully accountable for his actions. But that's not the total answer. Even individuals from good backgrounds get our sympathy.

The minute we use a person's environment as an excuse for misbehavior, *we are insulting and undermining the efforts of all those in similar circumstances who are living exemplary lives.*

Look at how the courts deal with our criminals. Almost everyone in our society claims to want tougher sentences, as crime is seriously eroding the quality of life all over our country. The judges running for election tell us they're "tough on crime," the district attorneys tell us they're "tough on crime," the police are "tough on crime," and the people themselves claim to be "tough on crime." Then why aren't we tough on crime?

How do the plea bargains and probations all come about? Why can't the combined will produce the results most everyone desires? Why are we more concerned with keeping a criminal out of prison than we are with keeping citizens safe?

This is not a liberal or conservative issue. Almost everybody favors tougher sentences for individuals fairly found guilty of wrongdoing. Yet we lack the will to punish.

If we can't discipline criminals, is there even a ghost of a chance we can discipline our kids? We have become unable to mete out a punishment that causes inconvenience, tears, or disappointment. It is so much easier to give a warning, and another chance.

On the rare occasion we do discipline, it disturbs us, even though we logically know it shouldn't. And we would rather have the poor behavior recur than live with the negative feeling we get when we enforce consequences. For although we talk tough to our kids, we mete out sympathy and understanding practically every time.

Look at the lack of will we display in our schools. As we all know, in some school districts guns and knives and assaults are part of the normal school day. This is America? And not just in bad neighborhoods, either. We can't even guarantee some of our kids a safe environment in which to learn.

We say that we value our kids' education, and want their time in school to be productive, but look what happens when our children's class has one or two kids who *always* cause disruptions. Often these children drive teachers crazy, understandably preventing them from giving their best. Further, by constantly disrupting, the troublemakers deny our kids a chance to receive the education our society has promised.

Just like the criminals in the court system, these children go on their merry way, and never are effectively punished. Threat after threat occurs, and not much is done. They still try out for the athletic teams and choir, and take part in the field trips and class parties. Most of our educators cannot come up with an answer for their behavior. Our kids suffer, and no one really cares enough to *solve* the problem.

Even if all the teachers, administrators, and guidance counselors uniformly agree that a disruptive kid belongs in a special class, in most cases the principal needs the parents' permission to make the placement. Many such parents refuse to agree, although that probably would be the best environment for their child.

Unfortunately, the School Board won't risk a law

suit from the parents by forcing the special placement. And the matter ends there. We stand by helplessly, allowing our kids to suffer daily as the disruptions continue.

The parents of the frequent disruptor always claim the child is going through "a difficult time," or perhaps there are "troubles at home." Even so, why must our children's education suffer? Aren't these the kids who need discipline the most?

If they *knew* they could be placed in a special class, without parental consent, might not their behavior improve? And when behaving students see nothing meaningful happen to the disruptors, what incentive do they have to behave?

Given all the problems in American homes, isn't the school almost impelled to be the disciplinarian of last resort? If discipline isn't practiced in the home, the kids' only chance is a school that cares enough to be tough. Yet the schools often preach understanding for students who desperately need to be disciplined, effectively denying them the key ingredient that might enable them to enjoy a life of quality and distinction.

We threaten and threaten, but never enforce discipline. We believe we're giving "second chances," but that's not true. Perhaps a hundred times in their lives, maybe thousands, these children have received "second chances" from people more interested in being liked than in helping. If all the previous threats didn't work, why do we naively think that the next one will?

Have you noticed a new term coming into our high schools and colleges, especially for athletes? Players now have a "history" of missing practices, or a "history" of having a bad attitude. This is where our lack of will leads. In the past, if kids had a problem, the coach saw that they *were* history.

Rather than punishing for unacceptable behavior, we often reward behavior that is ordinary. This is flawed. Do we want our kids only to act well when they are offered pizza and tickets to ball games?

In one school, administrators tackled the problem of discipline in the hallways in the following manner. Instead of reprimanding children who disrupted, the hall monitors gave out special certificates to those who behaved. At the end of the year, all the certificates were thrown into a bin, and if yours was selected, you'd win a prize.

We increasingly bribe our kids to act well, instead of punishing children when our standards are breached. It's easier to smile and give out trinkets than to risk unpopularity by being firm.

We parents often follow through no better. Would we have the problems today if we were tough and consistent? The disrespect our children sometimes hurl at us, the negative behavior toward others, the lack of achievement and respect for life?

A chief executive officer of a large company, an individual who orders around hundreds of people a day, can't for the life of him get his daughter to honor curfew. The hatchetman, who does all of his boss's dirty work, can't bring himself to take the toy away from his misbehaving child.

Why do so many of us need to be liked? It just doesn't come with the territory. If we want to be liked, we should give out dollars on street corners, but shouldn't expect to have a friendship with our kids. It's like vinegar and molasses, night and day. The minute we care if our children like us, we are theirs.

Remember the assistant principal in high school? If he was liked by the hoods, he just wasn't doing his job. He was paid to be tough, not sympathetic.

Recently when my son was in the hospital, part of his recovery program required him to breathe deeply into a tube to help keep his lungs clear. He especially liked the nurse who didn't require him to breathe deeply or frequently. He especially disliked one "tyrant," who required much more. Who was the better nurse? Simple, the tough one. She cared enough to be unpopular. And the same holds true for parenting.

We even go out of our way to make excuses for misbehavior. We say that it's a "hard time for our kids to grow up." This is of course true. But by saying this to our kids, aren't we giving them license to misbehave and claim their environment as an excuse? Isn't this all the *more* reason to be consistent and uncompromising?

Single-parent families understandably have special problems with discipline. When husband and wife both live in the same house, each can provide emotional support to the other. If mom gets mad at the kids, so what, dad's around to support her.

Unfortunately, many single-parent working moms have so little in their lives that their kids are their entire universe. It's hard to discipline when there is no one else in the home to provide emotional support. And even if the divorced parent remarries, often discipline still suffers. The step-parent commonly feels uncomfortable disciplining his spouse's kids.

An incident in California indicates the limits of discipline. A seven-year-old child stole twenty-five dollars worth of baseball cards, as well as several other items. The mother overreacted, and dressed the boy like a pig, tied his hands behind his back, sat him on a bench in front of his house, and painted his face blue. The child, wearing a pig nose, carried a sign on his chest which read, "I am a dumb pig. Ugly is what you will become every time you lie and steal."

The woman was cited for child abuse, and clearly her actions were excessive. But aren't all the parents who don't react to their children's misbehavior also in the wrong? Isn't their lack of disciplinary action almost as outrageous as this woman's behavior? Isn't it almost as harmful?

Until we can look beyond the tears and disappointment in our children's faces and discipline with firmness and lack of guilt, the troubles of our young will continue.

It is discipline and standards that can save our kids. The only question is, do we have enough love and will to impose them?

POINTS TO REMEMBER

- Discipline that is slightly too strict is better than no discipline.

- Popularity is for teenagers, not for parents.

- A second chance provided a troublemaker is more than likely his two-hundredth.

- Our sympathy should first be with the innocent victim, not the wrongdoer.

- Rewarding behavior that is only average will cause children to behave only when they are bribed.

- A child's home background may explain misbehavior, but it can never excuse it.

- The worse a child's home environment, the greater the need for effective, strong discipline.

- A disruptive, troubled child will always receive more attention than an average, behaving one.

- Criminals should get out of prison because they've served their time, not because of overcrowding.

- Punitive is not a four-letter word.

- A district attorney's salary should go down a hundred dollars for every plea bargain.

Keeping Kids Simple

*I*T SHOULD COME AS A SHOCK TO NO ONE that our "children of plenty" have plenty of problems.

Since showering our kids with possessions and attention isn't producing happiness, shouldn't we look at the pace at which we allow them to grow up? Shouldn't we slow it down, so that they have *less,* and therefore enjoy what they have *more?*

Look at the excesses all over adult society. We shop till we drop, and "do lunch" daily, as if having the right lifestyle automatically produces happiness. We spend money on nonsense like picture frames that talk, and radios that look like golf balls. One retailer actually sells sunglasses and hats for poodles, and many adults wouldn't be caught dead wearing the "wrong" label.

A Garfield holiday sweatshirt sums it up best, "Tis the season to be greedy." Even our cats are out of control.

Mail order catalogues are ever vigilant to satisfy our every need. Want some cold cuts? Dial 1-800-SALAMI 1. Want to pass your SATs? Dial 1-800-KAP TEST. We can just let our fingers do the walking, and what the heck, it's only money.

Kids have far more than they need. We read about young girls with thirty pairs of shoes, and two hundred dollar back-to-school dresses. Twelve-year-old boys have every baseball card ever printed, and tennis racquets that cost more than a hundred dollars.

Why can't we stop this dumping of possessions on our kids? Is there an unwritten law that kids must have it all, that children who do without are an embarrassment? It's clear what we're doing isn't raising happier children. Why is it so hard to try something new, to change our course, to experiment?

Middle-class children lacking the luxuries of their friends begin to perceive of themselves as poor, and feel sorry for themselves. An example of this occurred with my own son. Our home was a drop-off center for a food bank, and occasionally my son would see kind-hearted people ring our doorbell and drop off non-perishables.

After witnessing this for a week, he finally popped the question: "Is this food for us?" He thought that because we didn't have Atari or cable, we might qualify for the food.

What can we do differently, so that kids don't need

everything, so that they can be thankful for all that they do have in this land of plenty?

I have some ideas, but the cultural strength of the materialistic ethic is so strong, I am almost embarrassed to mention them. Most of the time my wife looks at me as if I'm crazy when I advance them, but of course she always looks at me that way.

Why not set up known age limits at which our children would begin to receive certain privileges or possessions? For example, dating could begin in high school. Ordering off the adult menu in restaurants could start at age twelve. Five-year-olds could get two TV toys a year. Wearing "in" clothing could begin at age thirteen. Kids would need to help with the cost of special activities that interest them.

Obviously we'd adjust the list to reflect our own priorities and values. Maybe toys aren't the problem, but licensed clothing is. Maybe we'll be liberal in one area, conservative in another. Regardless, by firmly establishing the age at which certain privileges occur, we won't be continually harassed by our kids. Whether they agree with our time-table or not, they'll come to accept it, and our lives will have been made all the easier.

Plus, the younger children will see their older siblings receive possessions and privileges on an ordered and planned basis, and won't be begging for them prematurely. They will become aware of stages in their childhood, and know that they won't "have it all" all of the time.

And imagine the excitement and joy when the landmark birthday finally arrives. The first expensive meal off of the adult menu, or the first shopping trip to get the licensed sweater will be something they never forget. And we can do everything possible to make the occasion special and memorable, an important and meaningful passage on the bumpy road to adulthood.

Look at how we take our kids to the movies. Often children see films advertised on one of their programs, and want to see them at once. My dear wife dutifully heads to the cinema, and it drives me crazy. Why pay five bucks a ticket, when in several months the movie will be at a budget cinema for a buck? Must children always get immediate gratification?

Most of our children never make it to the bleachers, as parents insist that they sit in the best seats available (that way they can distract the better element). Nothing upsets me more than hearing kids complain about their seats. Shouldn't they just be happy to be there? And don't dare try to show them how to save money by parking a mile away and walking to the game. The future track stars' legs can't take it.

Can't we keep our toys simple? Is bigger always best? The basic version becomes an embarrassment once the neighbor gets the deluxe variety, and even these kids, with tons of toys, are continually bored.

In Milford, Ct., the good citizens spent eight thousand dollars and constructed a skateboard track. The children didn't even use it—it's not "challenging" enough.

A child's published letter to Santa highlights the problem. This youngster wanted a racing set for Christmas, but not "some damn little two-track thing. I want something exciting." The more tracks our children demand, the more off-track they appear.

Recently a department store sponsored a promotion where young children could register to win a limousine ride to school on the first day. Do our first graders really need limousine rides?

Allowing youngsters to be world travelers while still in diapers is also self-defeating. Look at our own experiences. Did we see Europe at six months, or Jamaica at four? Were we the worse for it?

And distant family sojourns are by no means a sure recipe for happiness. Some families can go around the world and fight in every city, while others can go to a nearby motel for a weekend and have the time of their lives. Let's make travel to exotic places a stage of life for our children to look forward to, not the entitlement of toddlers.

And let's be strict with money. Extravagant allowances cause more harm than good. We must teach our children the value of money, and show them how saving occurs.

If we're planning a family vacation, why not take our kids to the Savings and Loan and make a deposit in a special account? Let them see how money accumulates. We might want to do this even if the cost of the vacation is not a burden for our family, just so our children learn how most people in the real world pay for trips.

And maybe we can ask them to contribute some pittance each month to the fund. If they think their money is helping pay for the vacation, they'll feel pride, and perhaps even have a more special time.

Even parents without financial concerns should encourage their children to work. Make them do chores for their allowance. If they don't keep up their end of the bargain, we won't keep ours.

Pay them for little "make work" assignments around the house, so they can begin to feel pride and reward for their efforts. If they want a special toy, or to be enrolled in a special activity, make them contribute to the cost. Perhaps we'll all be amazed how much less they ask for once they know that they need to help pay.

And try to keep main sources of money isolated. Nowadays, many fortunate children have sizable bank accounts. Perhaps there has been an inheritance from a grandparent, or holiday and birthday gifts of cash. Keep these funds separate, in a special account out of their reach.

By keeping our children's working capital small, the money they earn will have greater significance. If they have sixty dollars in savings, earning ten dollars mowing a lawn has meaning; if they have two thousand dollars, the identical job may appear meaningless, and won't produce the same sense of satisfaction.

Why do we insist on spoiling our children?

Perhaps one reason is the decline in family size. Years ago, families of seven and eight children were common. Since resources were limited, mom and dad needed to watch every nickel. Children would feel fortunate if a hand-me-down was in good condition. Now, families are smaller, and since we can often afford it, we find it hard to deny our children something they want.

Today's parents only recall the Great Depression through history books. We don't feel the same psychological motivation to save our money, and therefore we are more likely to allow it to be consumed by our kids.

And of course we have our guilts. Many moms work today, either because they need to or want to. And social problems like divorce make our kids' lives imperfect. As a result, many of us are predisposed to say "yes" to our children's requests.

TV certainly plays a role. It reaches into so many homes, all at once, that everybody wants the same thing at the *same time*. And through the tie-ins, with the toy manufacturers, cereal makers, fast food restaurants, and manufacturers of products ranging from bed sheets to squeeze bottles, the fad or product becomes *visible* everywhere we go. How can we expect children to avoid being caught up? Sometimes even we parents join in.

Perhaps we can't say "no" to our children because their role in the family has changed. We used to have more friends, and most of our relatives lived in our hometown. And almost always, two adults were present in every home.

Nowadays, society is tougher on relationships. Look at the rise of support groups. We have no one else to talk to.

As a result of our increasing isolation, I think often we view the family as a team, a "we" versus "they" in a cold, sometimes cruel world. Sure, we still need to discipline occasionally to remind the children who's boss, but it's as if parents and children are an emotional unit, providing strength and support to each other that used to be provided by others. Perhaps sometimes our children even take the place of friends we no longer have.

All this is especially tough on single parents. Little Lisa may be the only emotionally fulfilling human contact they have. Why create tension by disciplining her?

Most importantly, we seem to have developed an

irrational concern for our children's happiness. We *feel* for their every minor trauma. On a rational basis we know that life has its ups and downs, but on an emotional level, we have trouble extending this to our children.

The more insecure among us even try to gain status *from* our children. If the kids are dressed in the latest, and own the deluxe version of every hot toy, the folks are probably doing well. Why not let the kids advertise it?

And of course society in general has trouble disciplining. We prefer to react with understanding and compassion than with consequences. If we can't be punitive with our criminals, how can we be tough with a mildly mischievous loved one?

We cannot continue to shower our children with possessions. The Jones's kids may have fuller toy chests and closets, but unspoiled children will knock the designer socks off them in everything that is enduring and of value.

POINTS TO REMEMBER

- Children who have it all will appreciate nothing.

- We cannot spend ourselves to happiness.

- Parents who shop till they drop will have children who buy till they cry.

- Kids need thrills to look forward to, not possessions to look back on.

- The bleachers at baseball games are not just for adults.

- Kids who grow up too fast usually don't finish first.

- Raising a kind child is a more impressive accomplishment than raising an award-winning one.

Discipline That Fails

SOMETIMES IT SEEMS THAT WE HAVE AS MANY disciplinary approaches as we do children who misbehave. To spank or not to spank, to ignore a problem or treat it as significant, drive us to distraction. We've all developed our own styles, and pretty much think ours is the best approach.

The problem is that our discipline often isn't working. Let's look at the various approaches.

IGNORE THE PROBLEM

When it comes to their kids, many parents simply prefer to pretend the misbehavior isn't occurring. Perhaps this reflects a breakdown in shared values in our society. They can see that their child is taking skips in line, or is obviously disturbing others, but don't seem concerned. Often a child is practically falling out of a grocery cart, and his parents seem lost in outer space.

Only after *other* adults have noted the problem do they intervene. The child is told to stop roaming around the restaurant only after an icy stare from the fellow in the next booth, or the daredevil is cautioned that he is playing too rough only after an admonition from his playmate's parents. It's as if it is society's obligation to call inappropriate behavior to the parents' attention, and lacking that, the parents "see no evil."

LET THE KID LEARN

Here the parent divorces himself from the disciplinary function altogether, and lets the "free market" shape his child. The boy or girl learns that cheating is inappropriate by being caught, or that bullying is wrong by picking on someone stronger.

This "survival of the fittest" mentality has a couple of flaws. What about the meek, docile kids that this child takes advantage of? But the main defect here is that society doesn't discipline anymore, either. The child causing fights at school receives a wrist slap at best. He encounters no meaningful consequences.

If we are counting on society to do our disciplining, we should all wake up and smell the chaos.

REPEATEDLY SAY "DON'T DO IT"

Do you know folks like this? They *never* discipline, but talk a good game. They even appear and sound tough. If you didn't know better, you'd confuse them with disciplinarians. The scene usually goes something like this. A child is playing in a sandbox, and throws sand at her younger brother. Our concerned, efficient parent immediately jumps up from his bench, and tells his daughter "not to do it."

Eight seconds later, the behavior is repeated, and dad repeats his lecture. "I told you not to do it." This is spoken very slowly, and with great inflection and meaning.

At this point, the parent has bought twelve seconds of peace, before his daughter is at it again. He rushes over, as by now the younger brother is chest deep in sand and bordering on panic. He screams at his daughter, "I told you not to do it. How many times do I have to tell you?"

And it goes on and on like this throughout the afternoon. Dad never punishes the child for disobedience, but merely keeps repeating that she "shouldn't do it." He theoretically believes in discipline, but when push comes to shove, he just can't bring himself to "do it."

REASON WITH THE CHILD

Many parents find the act of discipline crass, and prefer to educate their little Freuds on the philosophical and psychological implications of their actions. The fact that they're two-and-a-half is irrelevant.

They probe with depth the meaning of all their kids' transgressions. Why did they do it? What were they thinking at the time? How do they think the other person felt? What does their behavior mean? Would they like to be treated that way?

Nothing is wrong with letting children know the implications of their actions, but if the negative behavior recurs, isn't a change due?

BE A FRIEND TO YOUR KID

This is a disease, an epidemic sweeping a great land. Parents try to be buds with their kids, even though they know that's not the way it should be. Were any of us buddies with our own parents? Would we have wanted to be?

Friendship and parenting do not mix. While it may be understandable why parents try to befriend their children, it is highly undesirable.

THREATEN A CONSEQUENCE BUT DON'T FOLLOW THROUGH

Some of the firmest advocates of discipline have this one down pat. They appear in control, but their kids are among the biggest disciplinary problems.

We might find their eldest child striking a friend. Our erstwhile hard-nose says to Billy, "Stop it. Your friend doesn't like it!"

Of course Billy persists. So the man of the house

yells, "Billy, you better stop it. There's going to be hell to pay if you continue."

Undaunted, Billy delivers an impressive uppercut, and the parent intervenes again. "Billy, there are going to be some severe consequences here. You don't want me to get mad, do you?"

At this point Billy again strikes his friend. "You're in trouble now."

Unfortunately, the parent never laid out for Billy what the specific consequences would be for his continuing misbehavior. Many times in the past dad had threatened and failed to follow through. Why should Billy think this time will be different?

Often unnamed punishments are deferred to the future. "Wait till I come back from my errand, young man, you'll really catch it." Or, "wait till we get home. All hell will break loose." In practice, dad returns from his errand and turns on the tube, forgetting to discipline, or the child falls asleep on the car ride home and all is forgiven by morning.

USE FAMILY CIRCUMSTANCES AS AN EXCUSE

How quickly we have become masters at this. If Shawn is having trouble at school, no problem, just blame it on the divorce. And it doesn't even matter when the divorce occurred. If the child was disruptive prior to it, he is "anticipating" the event. If he's naughty after it, he's having trouble "adjusting" to it.

We talk so much about the negative impact of divorce and other problems in the home that sometimes I think we are creating self-fulfilling prophesies. Often the guidance counselors at school, trying to be helpful, latch onto these events in the home as "excuses" for the kids' behavior. Kids become "children of divorce," even though this may not have been the initial cause of their misbehavior.

And we parents often tend to be very sympathetic towards our children during these times, and excuse misbehavior because "they're going through a rough time." Maybe we feel guilty because the kids' lives are not all sunshine and roses.

But isn't it at vulnerable times like these when discipline and standards need to be enforced most rigorously? Assuredly communicate with your children, discuss their feelings, perhaps consider a support group. But let them know misbehavior will not be received with a bias toward sympathy.

MAKE THE CHILD FEEL GUILTY

Don't all of us already have enough guilts? Some parents specialize in this type of approach. They don't really take anything away, but induce guilt.

They ask lots of rhetorical questions. "Is this the kind of behavior I get from you?" "How could you do this to me?" "I didn't think you were this kind of girl!"

Such a dangerous course, as perhaps the child will really begin to perceive herself as the rotten kid she's painted to be. And this will only make behavior worse.

YELLING AND SHOUTING

Many parents apparently feel that hysteria produces proper behavior. All of us have had the "pleasure" of seeing strong, silent types explode at their kids.

First, the face gets red, and veins pop out. Next, all self-control is lost, and they say things they don't mean. Fortunately for their blood pressure, such folks are usually slow to anger, and only erupt on occasion.

This won't change the misbehaving child. First, he probably enjoyed your little show. Maybe he and his brother have a bet on how many of your veins will pop out. Seeing you hysterical may make his day, proof positive of his impact as a person. Perhaps he's been goading you, just to get this response that you think he fears.

The danger here is that you will hit the child when you don't mean to, or say very hurtful things that he may never forget. Kids shouldn't see their folks out of control if it can be avoided. Sure, we're human, and have our off-moments, but it can be a very scary thing for a youngster to see.

Screaming can't be done everywhere. Outbursts are not appreciated in the middle of a movie theater or restaurant. So this form of discipline isn't applicable to all situations, and the fact that we *continually* need to shout indicates that it isn't working, either.

IT'S ONLY A PHASE

Don't you love this one? No reason to discipline the child; he'll outgrow the problem. So what if the world and its children need to suffer in the meantime.

No concern is shown for the people who have to bear the brunt of the misbehavior while the child "matures." And who says that when our child leaves one phase, he won't enter another? To be consistent, we'll have to ignore his behavior then, also.

BLAME THE SOURCE

Many parents respond defensively when they learn that their child has misbehaved. Remember the good old days when we actually believed the *teacher's* version of an incident? No longer. Now we give equal time (and credibility) to the kid. This is America, a democracy. And as often as not, we believe our child's version, though we can't quite figure out what this "biased" teacher has against our jewel.

SEND THE CHILD TO HIS ROOM

Used to be that this wasn't a bad little exercise. The kid might sleep, or listen to the radio (if he was lucky enough to have one in his room). Nowadays, rooms are pleasure palaces, with stereos, televisions, and video games. What kind of punishment is this?

If you're going to send your kid to his room, make sure the power is off. Otherwise, why not just take him to the video game parlor and call it a reward?

SPANKING

Except in specialized circumstances, spanking isn't the answer either. Mind you, it is a definite consequence for misbehavior, so it's at least presumably better than ignoring the problem. But there are limitations.

It can only be used at home. It's difficult to spank someone at the circus or in a crowded stadium. Further, what do we do when a child gets too old to spank?

And what of the danger of abuse? Given all the violence in our society, do we really want to be striking our own flesh and blood? I know that we do it out of love, but is this the best example we can give them? If we could find an equally effective method, wouldn't that be preferable? And there's always the risk that the person administering the discipline will flip out, and strike much more sternly than intended.

But as important as anything, spanking doesn't work. Everyone knows children who are continually being spanked. Sure, we inflict a little pain, but we don't take anything away from the child that he really wants.

DISCIPLINE, BUT GIVE IN
WHEN THE CHILD GETS UPSET

Some parents are perfect except for their follow through. If a child is misbehaving, they tell the child her behavior must change or there will be consequences. When she misbehaves again, the parent pronounces the consequences. So far all is fine, but it shortly falls apart.

The child cries, or threatens a tantrum, and swears the behavior will never recur, and incredibly, the seemingly strong-willed parent reverses himself. The punishment is rescinded, and negative behavior has been reinforced.

We can't stand to see our child upset. We try to mask our capitulation by telling her that she has "one more chance," but she knows better. She's won again.

Isn't it funny that many of us are so different at our jobs? There we supervise with military precision, and if anyone steps out of line, impose consequences at once. "That's what keeps everybody on their toes," we say. Yet we can't do the same at home.

Many of our kids never serve a *full* detention. If they are sent to their room for an hour, we feel sorry for them after twelve minutes. Or perhaps the neighbor kid comes over and wants to play. We always go with the fun, even though the disappointment of not being able to play would serve our child best.

DISCIPLINE, BUT NEVER TAKE AWAY ANYTHING MAJOR

Some parents only take away minor things, and never threaten the real core loves that would perhaps bring about permanent changes in behavior.

What if your kid loves cable? Let him know if a behavior recurs, it will be gone for two months. And let him pay for the re-installation. Or make him miss his Little League game. He'll survive. And if a child doesn't like the consequences we select, he may surprise us and actually behave.

DISCIPLINE ONLY TO YOUR CONVENIENCE LEVEL

What a wasted opportunity we have when we allow our own convenience to stop us from giving our kid a good lesson. If Kyle is in the middle of a restaurant, and is destroying our pleasure as well as that of all other diners, tell him he'll be taken home if his behavior persists. And see that it happens if it continues. Sure, he'll cry bloody murder, but so what?

For all of our threats, many kids have *never* been taken out of an event because they misbehaved. Never. Shouldn't we do this at least once, just to let our children know we occasionally mean business?

We can even stage this, where our convenience isn't an issue. If the child always is terrible in restaurants, we should stop at one sometime when we don't plan to eat. Order something inexpensive, and state the consequences for misbehavior. When the child acts poorly, whisk the lad home. It might just bring about proper restaurant behavior for a lifetime.

CLAIM YOUR CHILD CAN'T BE DISCIPLINED

Millions of people have already given up trying to control their kids. Rather than attempting to turn things around, they claim their child "can't" be disciplined. This has actually become quite acceptable and fashionable for parents to admit, as if they are secretly bragging about their kids' "free-spirit."

Our society will not achieve excellence as long as we are unable to discipline effectively. It is to that subject that we now turn.

POINTS TO REMEMBER

- Discipline without consequences is not discipline.

- Good parents discipline before the stares of others tell them it is necessary.

- One effective punishment is more valuable than twenty-two lectures.

- Threatening consequences without following through threatens our children's well-being.

- Better to ignore discipline entirely than fail to follow through with a promised consequence.

A Disciplinary Style That Works

SINCE MILLIONS OF OUR KIDS CONSISTENTLY misbehave and lack respect for themselves and others, how do we start the immense task of regaining control?

Believe it or not, the actual process isn't difficult—it has but a few steps. The issue isn't so much whether a new approach is required, but whether we possess the love and will to impose it. For we *can* get our kids back, but the task is up to us.

The disciplinary style presented here is based on several core beliefs and assumptions. If any of these are lacking, the ideas won't work.

HOMES SHOULD BE RUN BY PARENTS, NOT CHILDREN

I know this one seems ridiculous. Of course our homes are run by adults, right? Not really so, though it used to be true.

Today many children are treated like near equals, possessing rights and privileges beyond those of previous generations. Many parents are actually scared of their kids, and often the children set the rules for the entire household.

Look at what it's like in many homes. Young people are consulted about everything. Should we go to grandma's today? Can we go shopping for clothes on Saturday? The kids' schedule is what we work around, not vice versa. They can't miss a soccer game, but we can miss work or an appointment with a friend to drive them.

Homes are not meant to be democracies. Parents are Presidents, Senators, and Mayors all wrapped up in one. Of course our children should feel like they can discuss any subject with us at any time, but the buck stops here. Discipline is *our* show, the tone of the house is *our* responsibility, and the children are but bit players. It is our way, or no way.

PUNITIVE IS FINE

Parents who fear taking away privileges from their children should stop here. They will never be disciplinarians; they are too "kind." They should become resolved to lives of chaos and confrontation, and they shouldn't really complain, because they are partly the cause.

Why would discipline possibly be effective without

imposing substantial consequences when mis-behavior occurs? Kids aren't born with an innate disciplinary urge. From us they learn right from wrong.

Think of ourselves. If we speed, and get a ticket, that hurts our wallet and endangers our driving privileges. The penalty keeps us from the act. If the officer just lectured each time he pulled our car over, we'd ignore him, wouldn't we? Yet we try to "lecture" our kids all the time, when what's needed is a penalty.

Even though I'm suggesting a disciplinary style in which spanking has practically no part, I still may be accused by some parents of being "cruel." "How can we take important things away from our children?" they might ask. I would respond, "How can we have effective discipline without doing so?"

KIDS RESPECT TOUGHNESS

Do you think for a moment that our kids actually enjoy living amidst the chaos? The child who is a dis-cipline problem is secretly jealous of the disciplinary controls other kids complain of. He'd change places with them in a second.

No youngster will come out and tell us this, but every time we discipline effectively, we are showing our love and our care. Children know it inside, even if on an unconscious level. That's the way it's sup-posed to be—parents disciplining, kids complaining.

Ironically, it is by *not* disciplining that youngsters might begin to question our love.

If we watch some teenagers knock their parents sometime, we'll see the concept in operation. Each one has the "meanest old man in town." They complain about him, but their speaking up and even exaggerating his toughness is their way of bragging to the others that they are loved.

What if our kids hate the plan proposed here? Tough. Who said their opinion matters? It's whether the ideas work, not what they think. And why would we expect our kids to appreciate a firmer disciplinary stance? If they did like it, they'd keep it a secret anyway.

If we possess the will to discipline, it is a matter of a few simple steps to regain control of our homes and our lives.

INFORM YOUR CHILD OF THE CONSEQUENCES OF MISBEHAVIOR

We often don't do this. Incredible. We tell him how to act, but don't spell out the negative consequences that will occur for disobeying. We bore him with philosophical discussions about why his actions are wrong, which is generally unnecessary. Just by stating the consequences the child will know that we proscribe the action, and will almost intuitively know why.

We must be very specific when it comes to enunciating consequences for misbehavior. Spend some time before inaugurating the ideas here, thinking of a variety of suitable punishments, of varying harshness.

If your child swears at you, tell him that "if you swear at me one more time, you will miss your soccer game." Say it just like that. Let him hear the link between the inappropriate action and the consequence. Let there be no misunderstanding about what the consequence will be. To avoid problems, perhaps write down the penalties in a notebook, so that the child can't possibly claim that he was unaware of your position. Perhaps, both of you could initial the entry.

As much as possible, specify the consequences well in advance of the negative behavior possibly occurring. Don't worry, letting your kid know future consequences doesn't show you don't trust him. It just demonstrates that you want him to be aware he's always responsible for his actions.

Let's say your son is a new driver. Parents often give him the keys, tell him not to speed, and say a few prayers. Why not tell him that if he gets a speeding ticket, he needs to pay for it and loses his license for a month?

Yet because disciplining is difficult, many parents

avoid discussing subjects like this, hoping not to be confronted with the problem. And by *not* discussing the matter, the feared behavior is more likely to occur. Silence will not make it go away.

Specifying consequences is the most important element. Youngsters must know parents mean business if their behavior is going to change.

CHOOSE MEANINGFUL CONSEQUENCES

We musn't be sissies. Our children will not change if we threaten to take away items they don't care about. We know our kids best. Decide what's most important to them, and start there.

Not all of these need to be major. Kids never die from skipping a dessert. Forced writing actually works (today's generation just hates to write). Let the kids know that every time they swear, they must write "I will not swear" fifty times. This sounds terribly hokey, and it is, but if we do it, the swearing will be history.

Or get the kids in the pocketbook. Fines are very effective, as kids love their money. Perhaps impose a fine of a dollar a day if the room isn't cleaned by a certain time, and keep the meter running until the job is done. Or penalize the child fifty cents for every minute that he arrives home past curfew. You don't need to yell and chastise—just collect the cash.

TREAT DISCIPLINE AS A NORMAL, EXPECTED PART OF PARENTING

Enforce consequences in a matter of fact, unemotional manner. Don't lay tears, screams, and guilt on the child—you want to teach him, not make him feel worthless. If the consequence is a good one, you're doing more than thousands of screams could accomplish anyway.

Just simply tell your child the consequence, and be done with it. Enough said. It's no big deal. In fact, rather than feeling that you are *imposing* a consequence, let the child know that he is *choosing* it. He really is, you know. As long as you communicate that if something happens, a consequence will follow, he is the one who is deciding what will occur. If he decides to misbehave, that's *his* choice, and let *him* suffer the consequences.

You can even make this part of your original communication with him. "Mike, if you don't say thank you after opening each birthday gift, you can't play with any toy for two days. You decide which you would prefer. I'll be able to live with whatever you choose."

Don't make it seem like his misbehavior is unprecedented. Adults make mistakes, as most assuredly kids do. Tell your youngster that you were punished as a child, and it took you a while, also, to catch on to your folks' standards. Giving the disciplinary act more attention than it deserves makes it seem like a crisis rather than a normal part of growing up.

IMMEDIATELY IMPOSE THE PENALTY

It is essential that the consequence be imposed as soon as practical after the undesirable behavior occurs. If you told your child that the Nintendo would be taken away if he got an additional incomplete at school, take it away the instant you hear of his continued underachievement.

And don't make it a big deal. You are just carrying out your part of the bargain that he made with you. The kid made his choice, and has to live with the consequences.

This is why it is important to have a specific consequence already communicated to the child. You can avoid the screams, guilt, and hysteria when you learn that the misbehavior occurred, and just impose the penalty you previously announced.

If your child argues with you, and claims he didn't misbehave, ignore him. More than likely he's in the wrong. And if you once, or twice, *do* punish wrongly, your world will not fall apart.

But cover yourself. You can tell him that he's going to be punished, but if it is undeserved you are sorry. Or if you think that *perhaps* he is telling the truth, impose a less harsh consequence. But don't back away. Most kids will always claim innocence.

If you routinely let the child off the hook by "kindheartedly" giving him a second chance, he will know he is dealing with a paper tiger.

In order to avoid this human temptation to give the child a reprieve, be sure the consequence you enunciate is fair and realistic. If you yourself believe it is too severe, you might give in to a second chance rather than impose it.

RARELY LIGHTEN A CONSEQUENCE

Whatever consequence you are imposing, make sure the child lives up to it. If you say she will miss a TV show, make sure it's the whole show, not just half. If you said a week without Nintendo, don't cut it short after a day.

Many parents try to handle their guilt for disciplining by approaching their child and asking if "he's learned his lesson." The child automatically says "yes" and the penalty is terminated. Don't do this. If you do, the child will learn that you don't carry through with your consequences, and will constantly be asking you to cut the penalty short.

CONSISTENCY IS MANDATORY

The only way this system will work is if your child knows that you *always* follow through. If you punish the first time he swears, but ignore it the second and third, he has won, and you will still have the misbehavior to deal with.

If the action keeps recurring even after a punishment,

you have just two choices. Give up and ignore the problem, or make the consequence stiffer. The choice is yours—either you run your home, or let the kid do it.

IMPOSE CONSEQUENCES
EVEN WHEN IT'S INCONVENIENT

If you expect your children to behave when they are out with you, this is of especially critical importance. Let's say your family is visiting friends. Your children misbehave, and you say that if this continues you will take them home. Sure enough, history repeats. However, instead of leaving, you give them another chance, since you prefer to stay for one more cup of coffee.

The *best* lesson you can give your kids is to discipline even when it's inconvenient for you. This will show that you mean business wherever you are, and as a result, they will behave even when they are outside of your home.

PARENTS MUST BE UNITED
ABOUT DISCIPLINE

In a two-parent family, it is absolutely essential that the husband and wife agree on the disciplinary program they adopt. Perhaps one of them is a "softy" and can't bear to take something away from precious Lisa. Combine that with a spouse who loves strong discipline, and the kid will be getting mixed signals. Your efforts cannot succeed.

Clearly, the program isn't for all children. You can't communicate consequences to a three-month-old baby, but you'd be surprised how sophisticated your two-year-old is at avoiding negative consequences.

Also, some kids are beyond the point of parental help. They have become so embittered with their life, their family, themselves, that professional help is needed.

Remember, there are no perfect parents. My wife and I have made lots of mistakes with our kids, and perhaps you have too. Our children are more spoiled than some, and less spoiled than others. Everybody wishes they could get their kids to be better in certain ways. What's important is not to expect perfection, but concentrate and move forward doing the best you can. The answers won't always appear obvious, and to doubt yourself is human.

And all this does not have to be "negative." Reward your kids freely. If spelling is a tough subject, let them know that if they get three straight perfect scores, they can rent a movie, or a video game.

Or use something as a reward you would likely have given them anyway. Tell them that if they have no incompletes on schoolwork, they can go to baseball camp. Perhaps you were planning on sending them anyway, but they don't need to know that. Just remember that if they fail to perform, they have to hang up their spikes.

The more fun things you do with your kids, the better. Don't be just a grind; invest time to make their childhood memorable. Play catch, go swimming, picnic, whatever. By making this commitment, you are displaying the value you place on your children, and gaining the legitimacy in their eyes to be a disciplinarian. Your children will realize your penalties are motivated by love rather than revenge.

Let them know that a new day has dawned if you decide to use the ideas here. Sit them down, and tell them how it's going to be. Don't ask their permission, because *you're* the one in charge. But you might be able to answer their questions.

Obviously your kids will test you. Be prepared. The first time they challenge you is the most important. If you follow through, you're on the right road. If you waver, you're back to square one

Hopefully the ideas expressed here can help our kids maintain better control. Too many people in our society fail to be accountable for their actions. By working effectively at discipline, we will have a more peaceful home, and our children will have a better chance for happiness and success.

POINTS TO REMEMBER

- If our children aren't upset with the consequences we impose, we should toughen them.

- Parents who fundamentally disagree about discipline will have children who misbehave.

- Homes are not democracies.

- The more punitive the consequence, the less likely parents will need to impose it.

- All kids want discipline, whether they say so or not.

- We don't impose consequences; our children elect them.

- Effective parents rarely give second chances.

- The more fun we have with our kids, the less they will misbehave.

APPLICATIONS

Introduction

*T*HREE SECTIONS ARE PROVIDED TO ILLUS-
trate these ideas in practice. Each relates to children
of a particular age range. But read all three. Perhaps
the problem that concerns you is dealt with in a
different section than you might think. Also, by seeing
varying consequences presented, you are more likely
to find one that might be helpful in your disciplinary
approach.

It is our job as parents, or grandparents, to decide
which penalties and rewards to apply when. All kids
are different, as are all parents, so please adjust these
concepts to your own needs. You know your kids
best.

Are these final answers? Of course not. The illus-
trations merely serve as a guide to suggest possible
paths that might lead to a home of greater peace.

Applications:
Birth to Age 5

*C*LEARLY, NEWBORNS ARE HARDLY ABLE TO
conform to our wishes. Babies are wholly dependent,
and can't exercise much control over their actions.
Yet by the age of one-and-a-half or two, children well
understand the concept of punishments, and can be
expected to be held accountable for their actions.

They may not always let on, but our young are a
lot smarter (and sneakier) than we give them credit
for. So we mustn't delay discipline until they reach
some arbitrary age; we must start to enforce standards
at the first instant we believe they can fairly be held
accountable for their actions.

My Child Won't Say Thank You When She Gets a Present

We parents have few higher obligations than turning
our children into thoughtful, respectful adults. Don't
let your child get away without saying "thank you."

Tell her that if she doesn't say "thank you" when opening a present, the gift will be taken away for a week. And don't relent. After seven days, she will have learned her lesson. If not, repeat the punishment at the next opportune occasion. Remember, regardless of what they say, grandparents do like to be thanked for their gifts!

Do the same for the horrible "I have it already" that kids often utter when opening a present. Warn about the consequences, and explain why such behavior is inappropriate. If they persist, you persist with your discipline.

My Child Bites Other Children

Again, action is required. Don't just tell your daughter that biting is bad, but tell her specifically what will happen if she bites again. Make it stiff.

How about a week without Sesame? Or two weeks without her favorite doll? Or maybe slap her hand five times when the behavior recurs, and tell her she will receive five additional slaps each time this happens again.

Pick whatever you think will best motivate her to stop this dangerous habit, and always remind her of the consequences prior to her playing with other kids. Hopefully, in a short time she will have the concept down pat.

My Child is Difficult to Get out of Bed in the Morning, and Dressing Him is a Pain

Every child has a different internal clock, but if this is upsetting you, take some action. Particularly since so often mom now has to get to work in the morning, problems here are especially frustrating.

Perhaps give the kid a countdown from twenty, and if he is not out of bed by then, a consequence will follow. Or play this game. Give him to twenty, but let him earn a "point" for each second before twenty that he is out of bed. When he gets to fifty points, he can get a treat.

If he doesn't cooperate when you dress him, leave the room if time allows. In fact, if he doesn't need to be dressed that day, let him remain in pajamas as a "punishment." Or make him miss breakfast. He won't die. That's preferable to starting each day with tension and screams, isn't it?

My Child Cries at Length When I Discipline

What did you expect, applause? Perhaps this sounds cruel, but kids don't have an inalienable right to lengthy crying spells. Of course, if your children have nightmares, or any other legitimate reason for crying, don't cut them off. But many kids cry just for the effect. They know that in a crowded restaurant tears turn adults into marshmallows, and they will be given second chances.

SPOILED ROTTEN . . .

If you think your kid is crying for effect, tell him to knock it off. If he continues, tell him if he doesn't stop, the punishment will be doubled. Believe it or not, it works, which probably proves the crying was for effect in the first place.

Perhaps once or twice in five years you might make the wrong decision, and cut off the tears prematurely. Either you can lose sleep about it, or remember that you are an excellent parent most of the time, and that you never promised your kid perfection. And because these crying scenes will become increasingly rare, you will become an even better parent in the process.

My Child Calls Other Children Names

This is common enough, and presumably not hard to solve. Don't lecture each time about how cruel it is to call the overweight child "fatso." Perhaps every time he namecalls, spend the whole day calling him that same name.

Or if that seems immature to you (which it probably is), let him know the punishment that follows each time he acts so rudely to his friends. If the consequence is appropriate, the habit will soon disappear.

My Child Always Acts Badly at Birthday Parites

So make him miss one; he'll survive. If he were sick and needed to miss a party, life would still go on.

160

BIRTH TO AGE 5

Let your child know that if he is naughty, he will be taken home. Don't be concerned about embarrassing him. If he has it coming, just do it.

Don't worry about the birthday boy being "sad" if his friend needs to leave early. He'll forget all about him at the first sign of the cake.

My Child Always Runs into the Street Without Looking

This is heavy stuff. Your child could be seriously injured, so nothing is more important. Save the lectures on pedestrian safety, and slap your child on the hand as many times as necessary until he gets the concept.

Perhaps enforce this spanking with other communicated penalties. Tell him there's no television for a week, or call off a special trip with grandma. But if you are going to be tough in one area, please do it here.

My Child Interrupts When I Am Talking on the Phone

Your child can easily learn that this is wrong. Just enforce a consequence each time it occurs.

Let the youngster sit quietly near the phone during an actual conversation, to make sure she understands the concept.

And perhaps make it all a game. Tell her that for every phone call she doesn't interrupt, she gets two points. When the total reaches twenty-five, give her a treat. And keep a running score on the fridge, so she can see how close she is to the reward. Always make her go back to zero if she interrupts.

In a short time she will learn the appropriate behavior, and the game will be forgotten.

My Child Doesn't Play With His New Toys

Most kids don't, except when a friend wants to. Require your child to play with any new toys he asked for. What better way of getting him to understand that he assumes a responsibility when requesting a plaything.

My Child Wants to Decide What He Wears

Isn't this too bad for the little dear? You are running the house, not he.

Tell him the way it is, and dress him accordingly. If he protests, too bad. Take away a garment if he is uncooperative, or strike a compromise. Two days a week he picks his wardrobe, five days you do. If you allow a toddler to dictate his wardrobe, you are only opening yourself up to horrendous problems with fashion later.

My Child Won't Share

No kid wants to share. Many adults aren't wild about the concept, either.

Perhaps tell her that every time you see her share, there's a reward. Make it minor, but let her know the considerate behavior is appreciated. A special trip to the park in honor of her sharing is always in order.

If this doesn't work, take something away from her each time she doesn't share. Whether she likes it or not, she'll eventually get the concept. The sooner you can end irritating practices such as these, the easier and more fun your job of parenting will be.

My Child Misbehaves in Restaurants

Some kids have trouble with this. They simply can't sit still. You can only require proper behavior once you're convinced your children are capable of it.

What are you prepared to do to penalize them for misbehavior? Clearly, kids can get impatient in restaurants, so do your best to entertain them at this time. But let them know there are limits, and the consequences that will follow if they don't stay within them.

My Child is Terrible in the Grocery Store

Parents often can't quite find the formula to assure cooperation here. This is unfortunate, since food shopping is a sufficiently irritating experience without a child adding to it.

First, if you plan on getting your little one a treat at the check-out lane, only do so if he's been good.

If you can't bring yourself to deny him his precious treat, why *should* he behave?

If your child always begs you to buy certain brands, tell him beforehand which product, if any, he can make the decision on. If he demands more input, put the item back on the shelves. He won't like it, but that is how he'll learn.

Play an innocent game or two. Give him a point for each aisle he's perfect. If there's fifteen aisles in the store, tell him he needs fourteen points to get a treat. Maybe count the weeks he's been perfect in a row, and tell grandma and your friends so he can feel proud of his accomplishment.

* * * * * * * * * * * *

Transforming newborns into behaving five-year-olds is tiring and exhausting. By imposing consequences for misbehavior, we will find more of our time filled with fun rather than tension. And as we look back on these wondrous first years of life, we will be repaid with a multitude of wonderful memories.

Applications: Ages 6-13

*T*HE OLDER CHILDREN GET, THE MORE LIKELY they are to test us, to see if we seriously believe in the standards and behaviors we've tried to establish. Be prepared for the onslaught, and be especially tough. Remember, we're not trying to take the fun out of family life; we're trying to put it in, by making sure poor behavior doesn't ruin opportunities for joy and unity.

My Child Doesn't Do His Chores Around the House

This is a direct challenge to your authority. Remind your youngster of the consequences for not fulfilling his obligations. Maybe hold back a week's allowance, or triple the chores the following week. He'll get the message quickly enough if you hold firm.

Try not honoring one of your obligations. If he can decide not to clear the table, you can decide not to drive him to the movies. Let him realize that every parent has tons of chores around the house, and they must be done even if they're not fun. So too for him.

My Child Swears Around the House

Make sure you want to confront this. The truth is that kids today speak a lot differently than we did at their age. Their friends aren't shocked by the language, and often the less made of it, the better.

But if you feel it is important to create changes, here's a fun way to do it. Impose a fine of twenty-five cents each time you hear a swear word. This can go towards a future family outing. Keep track on a sheet of paper how much money each family member owes. This works, believe it or not. The other kids will snitch when Katie says the F word, and you will be amazed how quickly speech patterns change. Even dad's language might improve!

If your children swear *at* you, then you have a more severe problem. I can't imagine allowing children to do this. If you don't react, you're allowing them to run your house.

How do we get rid of the problem? Think of something terribly substantial to take away the next time this occurs. Of course warn of the penalty ahead of time, so they can't claim they didn't know the consequences. Make them miss a month of TV or take away telephone privileges. Whatever it is, you cannot allow this to continue. You are far too valuable to be spoken to in this manner.

My Child Watches Too Much TV

Why not set limits? So many minutes a day. Keep track on a chart, and don't go back on your word.

Perhaps tie TV time to reading time. Require reading during commercials. Or perhaps just allow an hour a week, but give additional time based upon pages read.

You might want to tie TV viewing to other activities, also. Every half hour watched might require three trips around the block by bike. You'll be amazed how this can minimize TV viewing. And even if it doesn't, at least the children will be in better physical shape.

To make viewing a little less desirable, decree that no eating can occur in front of the set. Watch, it's amazing how habits will change. And you'll save a fortune on junk food.

My Child Disrupts in School

Here you are being tested. Roll over and play dead or strut your stuff. Talk with the teacher, and tell him to inform you the minute such behavior recurs. Let your child know of this conversation, and the consequences for a continuation of this unacceptable behavior.

Perhaps take away the skateboard, or the ballet slippers. If you don't act decisively here, your child won't be learning, and may get a bad rap that will follow him through school.

My Child May Be Experimenting With Alcohol

Alcohol is becoming an ever bigger problem for parents to deal with. Tell your children what the strong consequences are for trying alcohol. Almost everyone experiments with it before they hit the legal drinking age, though hopefully not in this young age range.

Keep as little alcohol in the house as possible. If you rarely drink, buy pints rather than quarts when entertaining, and perhaps even pour out the leftovers after your guests leave, so your kids have less temptation.

One of my children recently wrote a report on AA, and we went down to the local office to pick up some literature. This was a sobering experience. Take your kids there, or even to a meeting. Let them begin to see how much misery alcohol causes.

My Child Leaves Dirty Dishes All Around the House

If this aggravates you, have some fun. Keep a chart in the kitchen of the number of dishes you discover in bedrooms or closets. For every ten, maybe you can receive something, like breakfast in bed or a car wash.

Moms and dads are not maids, and the sooner the kids realize it, the happier everyone will be.

My Child is Frequently Tardy in School

Don't explode at him when this occurs—just impose a penalty. Maybe show up late at the events he considers important. You'll know what's best. Monitor his progress on the next report card, and have your child know you've told the teacher to call you whenever it recurs.

My Child Leaves His Bike Unlocked Outside, and Leaves His Toys Out for the Night

Kids can have trouble learning responsibility. Impose a fine every time this occurs. Or perhaps withhold use of the bike or toy for a certain length of time. After all, if these items would have been stolen, they would have done without them for good.

My Child Gets Incompletes at School

Tell your child that this is *unacceptable*, and impose consequences at once. Obviously check if he needs a tutor, or eyeglasses, or if there are problems in the classroom. But once the kid starts this habit, it is a difficult one to break.

My Child Doesn't Read Enough

Why not require a change? Go to the library frequently with your kid, and sit and read. And if reading is hard for him, all the better to practice.

Maybe link reading to his activities. If he doesn't read a book a week, no Little League, or piano lessons, or gymnastics. All our kids would read more if we forced them to.

Try installing a family reading period in your home. Pick one or two nights per week, and let the whole family spend a required hour reading whatever they like. Perhaps assign a different family member to select a treat each time which can be enjoyed as you all sit around together reading. This is an incredibly pleasant experience.

My Children Always Fight Over Who Gets to Go First, or Sit in the Front Seat

Here's the solution. Pick some arbitrary formula that automatically determines which kid gets the honor. For example, if you have two kids, alternate months. In January, March, May, July, September, and November, Billy is the big shot. In the other months, his sister is. This avoids countless arguments.

My Child Drives Me Crazy About Licensed Clothing

Anticipate this problem. It will always come up.

If you can, set an age at which licensed clothing will be allowed. No GAP clothes till age fourteen, or whatever. And stick to it. And let your youngster know that every time he asks prematurely, he'll have to wait two additional months.

If you *have* to get the licensed stuff, make your child pay for part of it. You might contribute what a pair of "normal" jeans would cost, and let him make up the difference. Or give him a clothing allowance each month, and force him to allocate it. He might not buy the licensed sweater for twice the price if it means having half the wardrobe.

My Child Always Argues Endlessly When He Doesn't Get His Way

Don't let him. Disciplining won't bring peace and relative order if you allow hours of complaints every time you take action.

The child possesses no innate right to do this to you. Make your decision, or impose your consequence, and that's it. If your child carries on excessively, tell him that if you hear one more word on the subject, you'll impose additional consequences.

Perhaps this is why some parents never effectively discipline their children—they don't want to put up with the tantrums that result. So don't take any crap

SPOILED ROTTEN . . .

from your kids when you make a decision. You're in charge.

My Child is a Poor Sport

Don't excuse this by saying "it's in the kid's nature." Create change. It's easy.

I witnessed a remarkable demonstration of this one recent weekend when I was bowling. On the next lane, a child stamped his foot every time he did poorly. It was appalling to watch.

After a time, the parent had had enough. She told her son that there would be a fine every time he did this. It was a wonder to watch. With the very next miscue, the child was ready to kick the floor but remembered in time. And from then on there were no outbursts.

With all the examples of athletes who are poor sports, let's try doubly hard to see that our children don't follow in their footsteps.

My Child Acts Terribly Whenever We Make a Car Trip

By using rewards and punishments, you might be able to create some helpful changes.

I recently read of one mom who devised a wonderful system for avoiding the inevitable, "When will we get there?" She gave each child a roll of quarters at the beginning of the trip. Every time they asked

"When will we get there?" they had to give back a quarter. Sounds ingenious.

Or use points as a reward. "Grade" your children every half-hour. If they have enough points at the end of the day, perhaps the family can go to a fancy restaurant for dinner. But if they don't, eat elsewhere. Or maybe you'll treat them to a water park if they earn enough points.

Be prepared to stay in the motel with a misbehaving child while your spouse and the other kids go out to have fun. This will provide a permanent lesson, and future car trips should be much more pleasant for the whole family.

*   *   *   *   *   *   *   *   *   *   *

By maintaining standards throughout these years, we give our children a much better chance of surviving their teen years intact. Many temptations will come their way. The tougher and more loving the regimen they're used to, the better prepared they will be to resist them.

Applications:
Ages 14-19

*T*HESE YEARS ARE OFTEN THE STORMIEST AND most traumatic for kids and their parents. With all the problems in society, we often feel fortunate if our children survive these years relatively unscathed.

We should remember that we weren't perfect as teens, either, and assure our children that our love is there even when they don't live up to our expectations.

My Teenager Dresses Funny

Tough. Your teen's appearance is no reflection on you. He won't look like that when he is twenty-five (please God), so keep things in perspective. The more you criticize the "look," the longer he will keep it.

You might just drive him crazy, however, by saying that his appearance is growing on you. Nothing will get him to change faster.

My Teenager May Be Using Drugs

All kids are potential drug users in high school—yours, mine, and everyone else's. I have an idea; it's a little controversial, but I think it's worth doing.

So often you see parents driving themselves crazy over their teen's possible drug use. Yes, he's acting strangely, but is he or isn't he doing drugs? And by the time they get up the nerve to ask, the answer is a lie and the damage has been done.

Aren't the issues here so important that parents should insist upon a drug test at the first suspicion? Yes, your child will resent it, but does that make it wrong?

You may feel uneasy that you are forcing your child to testify against himself. But won't standing by and watching him self-destruct make you feel even worse?

My Teenager Had a Minor Scrape With the Law

Don't be in such a hurry to help him out. If he's in jail, let him spend the night. If he's not, have him tour the jail, so he can see what it is like.

Punish him for his actions. If you sensed this was coming, better to have announced the consequences previously. Regardless, be tough, let him know you mean business, and tell him what will happen if this recurs.

AGES 14-19

My Teenager Won't Get a Job

Discuss your expectations for work. If she doesn't like fast food restaurants, tough—tell her to find something else. Perhaps match some of the money she will earn, and put it into the college fund. But at all costs, be sure she mixes with other people and learns how the world works.

The same with mowing lawns and babysitting. *Make* your kids do this. It is not an option. And if they don't perform their duties in a responsible manner, nail them. If they can slough off on their first job, why wouldn't they continue to do so on their next?

My Teenager Uses the Telephone Too Much

Set some standards, and stick to them. There are other members of the household, and they need to be respected. Perhaps set up a known time period each night when your teen can't be on the phone. He will communicate it to his friends, and at least there will be some peace.

A phone is important, and that's how your child stays in contact with his friends. But allowing him to think he's lord of the manor will do no one any good.

My Teenager Drinks Alcohol

Again, a tough one. You want him to know it is wrong, but you also want him to feel he can call you for a ride if he is drunk. In fact, if he calls you, I can't see how you can punish him.

Stressing how often kids become alcoholics may help, and keeping an eye out for telltale signs is a requirement. All you can do is hope that his upbringing will keep him tolerably in control during these years.

My Teenager Wants to Take a Year Off After High School

Is this so bad? The older the student, the more he gets out of the college experience. Just don't support him for the year. Make sure he is working. Check out his source of income if he seems to have none; he may be dealing drugs.

Agreeing with the teen that he should take off a year is often the best guarantee that he will change his mind.

My Teenager Is Having Sex

So many adults have different views on this subject, it's almost impossible to write anything that won't upset someone. Again, as much as you want to convey the right and wrong of sexual behavior, you also want your teen to know that his place in the family is secure and that your love will always be there, no matter what.

One idea might be to take your kids on a tour of

the maternity section of the local hospital. Have them look long and hard at the newborns. Describe the responsibilities babies entail, and point out how their freedom would be destroyed by having to care for one. Perhaps have teen moms (or dads) give a talk at the high school, describing their experiences.

Even with all the social diseases, the trend toward relatively early sex seems as strong as ever. Informing your teenager about all aspects of sex, and reminding him of the awesome burdens of parenthood, may be your best defense.

My Teenager Can't Hold a Job

Some kids try to lose jobs on purpose, all the better to be home or at play. Tell your daughter ahead of time that if she "quits" her job, you will call the boss to find out why. She may resent this, or be embarrassed, but tough. It might just keep her on track.

My Teenager Is Driving Me Crazy About the Car

Driving is one of the most exciting changes that marks these years. Suddenly your son has the freedom to go where he wants, in convenience and style.

The car should be used as a reward and penalty.

Tell him that if he doesn't meet certain realistic grade requirements, he won't be allowed to learn how to drive. Link continuing use of the car to behavior or educational performance, so that he has a strong incentive to obey and stay on track.

Make him responsible for his driving record. If he's caught speeding, have him pay the fine. If the insurance goes up as a result, have him pay that, too. Have your insurance agent inform him of the increased premiums that will result from an accident. And continually remind him how dangerous a car can be, and of the problems caused by drunk driving.

Your kid loves the car. If he is not behaving, deny him use of it. If that won't straighten him out, perhaps nothing will.

My Teenager Always Comes Home Past Curfew

By imposing penalties, you should be able to handle this. Perhaps play a game, where if ten straight curfews are honored, the curfew becomes later. Or say that for every minute of late arrival, that's how many days your daughter goes without the car.

My Teenager Runs With a Terrible Crowd

You have limited control here. Perhaps encourage the child to join different groups where she will meet new people. If her friends are pure deviants, perhaps you can forbid the association. But parents often exaggerate how bad their kid's friends are, and perhaps it's a better group than you think.

Remember to impose penalties for misbehavior in general. This will perhaps limit the negative influence of the group.

My Teenager Plays the Stereo Too Loud

This is easy. After one warning, take the stereo away for a certain period of time. If you find the kid ever plays the stereo too loud again, take it away for three times longer.

My Teenager Lies to Me

I guess all kids do occasionally. Probably don't make too much of it until you are sure you see a pattern. Then, let the consequences fly.

My Teenager's Grades Are Poor

Impose consequences quickly. However, be sure your expectations are realistic.

Let your child know that if he doesn't achieve a certain grade point, he will be deprived of use of the car. Perhaps his allowance will go down, or he'll need to miss an athletic event. Whatever you decide is the motivator, enforce it, and just watch the improvement. But of course be ready and willing to help him achieve the grades you agree to.

* * * * * * * * * * *

Regardless of how hard it is to believe, most kids survive their teen years, and go on to normal lives. How they treat their spouse and their kids, however, will in part have been determined by us. By being loving, strict, and imaginative, we will give our children an excellent basis for a life of happiness, success, and meaning.

FINAL THOUGHTS

Questions and Answers

If you've made it this far, you may have some questions. I've tried to anticipate a few.

What gives you the right to suggest these ideas?

Good question. I'm not a shrink or cultural theorist. But I am a parent, one who feels desperately that our children need to change. The work ethic is dying, underachievement is becoming respectable, and drug and alcohol abuse are skyrocketing.

Perhaps we parents have waited too long for the experts to solve the problems. We know our kids best. Why not organize, share ideas, put forth some solutions, and have a fighting chance to lessen the problems? By getting involved and working *with* the experts, maybe we'll achieve the best results for our children.

But in final analysis, my background isn't what

matters. What matters is whether I've accurately described some of our young, and whether the suggestions offered here are on target.

You talk about children being spoiled, yet aren't there millions of kids living in poverty?

You're right, most of my experience is with middle-class kids, so some of what is said may not apply. But certainly much does.

Demanding consequences for misbehavior is an appropriate policy for all children, regardless of income level of the family. And often it is the least wealthy homes which are characterized by the poorest discipline.

Even in low-income families, many children don't perform outside jobs, and if they do, enthusiasm and achievement are often lacking. And the minute the folks get money, you know the kids will be demanding and receiving all the TV toys they now are denied.

Are our kids really this spoiled? Didn't you show us a stereotype?

Yes I have, but like any stereotype, parts of the description are true. Maybe your child studies hard but still is a slave to fashion, or is thoughtful and considerate but can't hold a job. Excess is so commonplace that it is a rare child who is not affected.

Isn't this stuff pretty negative, with all this talk of consequences? Kids need fun, too, don't they?

Of course they do. Show it to them. Not only is that your responsibility as a parent, but it makes your disciplining easier. Without a doubt, good parents will have an easier time with this program.

What about peer pressure? What if all my son's friends are doing something? How can I deny him?

It's not easy, but you'll find a way. The best cure for peer pressure is to be an excellent parent, and let your child know all that he has that his friends don't.

But independently, tell your son you don't care what other parents do, and make this clear from an early age. Stress how many kids grow up with problems, and indicate you plan to avoid it.

And always check with his friends' parents to see if your son is correct in describing reality. Is everyone going to Mexico, or just one person? Does everyone date, or just one girl? Did Bobby really get a new car, or a three hundred dollar lemon?

If you allow your child to do something just because a classmate can, you are perhaps allowing the worst parent in the class to set the performance standard for the grade.

Won't imposing these ideas cause hostility?

It might. So what. Explain the program to your child as clearly and as calmly as possible. If he feels hostile because you are meting out consequences, it shows the importance of gaining control. Prisoners aren't in love with their jailers, and your child doesn't have to feel grateful for every consequence. You're running things, not he.

What is the most important part of the plan?

Being consistent. Announcing a "new day" in discipline is absurd if you offer a consequence-less tomorrow. This is the key, the absolutely mandatory element. If you get lazy with follow-through, *you're* through, and your kid will be back running your household.

My child is already 18.
Is it too late to make some changes?

If the child lives away from home and you provide no financial help, sure it's difficult. But you can always communicate expectations, and express disappointment when they are not met. If you are providing financial help to your child, the likelihood of success increases.

What's wrong with giving a kid what he asks for?

Nothing. The problem comes up when his every wish is fulfilled. Treats are perceived as entitlements, and through their abundance, aren't enjoyed.

Isn't this program one-dimensional,
just concentrating on consequences?

This is a fair thought, since obviously that's the emphasis. The advantage here is that the child knows where he stands, and what consequences will occur if he misbehaves. As a result, his behavior will likely be appropriate.

No one is opposed to trying to understand *why* children act the way they do, and clearly the more you communicate with your youngsters about feelings, the better. If a child feels scared in his room, try to reassure him, and obviously don't mete out consequences. Many times you'll react in this manner. If possible, *always* try to find out the root cause of the behavior.

But sometimes it is almost impossible to know why a child acts a certain way. Often he doesn't know himself. Rather than getting bogged down in deep analysis of every misbehavior, better to impose a consequence and see if the behavior disappears.

Aren't larger problems in society a cause of some of our kids' misbehavior?

Of course. Alcoholism, child abuse, and poverty wreak havoc daily. But these problems have no quick, easy answers. Does it make sense to put our standards on vacation for twenty-five years while society tries to get itself in shape? Because many homes are having difficulties, isn't that a reason society *needs* to enforce its standards?

What extra responsibilities do parents have in this?

Lots. Set the example. If you are a slave to fashion, your kids will be too. If your children see you drinking excessively, why wouldn't they be heavy drinkers? If you are negative and frustrated by life, why wouldn't this rub off?

Be independent. Occasionally deny your children the toy their friends have. Find the strength to set dollar limits on their clothing purchases, and to see that they get what they need, not necessarily what they want.

Most of all, don't give up. It is so easy to accept mediocrity that we sometimes forget what excellence is like.

I recently was talking with a manager of a fast food restaurant, and he commented he received many complaints from customers about service. Defensively, he asked me, "Do you know how hard it is to work with kids today?"

The minute we ignore our standards because effective management is hard work, we have lost. Somehow Disney World and most of our successful theme parks function perfectly, with the *same* batch of teenagers maintaining immaculate grounds and providing courteous service.

We must have the courage to risk the temporary unpopularity that comes to those who don't compromise their standards.

Is This Working?

ARE THE IDEAS PRESENTED HERE WORKING? Are they helping with your children? Do you agree that many of our kids are out of control, or am I perhaps being unfair?

What consequences do you use? Have a particularly effective one? What is *your* style of discipline?

I'd love to hear from you. Please write with your reactions and ideas. P.O. Box 11558, Milwaukee, Wi 53211. After all, by communicating and working together, we can provide our kids the best possible chance for a life of happiness and value.

Conclusion

WE MUST BEGIN THE PROCESS OF TAKING back our children. Conceptions of work, value, and discipline must be restored. We must give our children what they need, not necessarily what they want.

The excuses and excesses must stop. Consequences must follow misbehavior. That's how the world has always worked, and is doubtlessly how it shall function in the future.

Football offers instant replays, but life does not. We should take charge of our children's lives today. They are with us for such a short time, yet the values and ideals they internalize become not only their lifetime habits, but those of *their* children as well.

Give them standards to believe in, and let them see that these are so important that we discipline for their breach.

Concentrate on *their* character rather than licensed ones. We must love them more but simultaneously surround them with less. An occasional T-shirt may be plain, or a toy chest half empty, but our children will be fulfilled, and future prospects enhanced.

The world's largest company is no longer IBM or AT&T, but Nippon Electric. Japan gives away more foreign aid than the United States, and we have become the biggest debtor nation on earth. Toyota has sold more Corollas than Ford, Model T's.

America will rise to greatness once again, but most assuredly not on a diet of second chances and unenforced standards. We must take action, now, together, if most of our children are to experience the America we had, and the one we so fervently wish for them.

We should not, and cannot, wait any longer. The time for change is NOW.